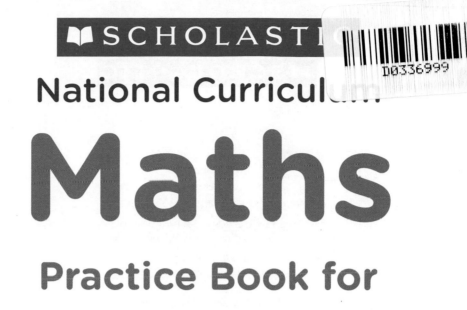

National Curriculum
Maths
Practice Book for

Year 4

Book End, Range Road, Witney, Oxfordshire, OX29 0YD
www.scholastic.co.uk

© 2014, Scholastic Ltd

11 12 13 14 15 16 17 18 19   4 5 6 7 8 9 0 1 2 3

British Library Cataloguing-in-Publication Data
A catalogue record for this book is available from the British Library.

ISBN 978-1407-12891-7
Printed by Bell & Bain Ltd, Glasgow

Editorial
Rachel Morgan, Robin Hunt, Kate Baxter, Lesley Fletcher

Design
Scholastic Design Team: Neil Salt, Nicolle Thomas
and Oxford Designers & Illustrators Ltd

Cover Design
Neil Salt

Illustration
Aleksander Sotirovski

Cover Illustration
RA Studio

Contents

Why buy this book?

The *100 Practice Activities* series has been designed to support the National Curriculum in schools in England. The curriculum is challenging in mathematics and includes the requirement for children's understanding to be secure before moving on. These practice books will help your child revise and practise all of the skills they will learn at school, including some topics they might not have encountered previously.

How to use this book

- The content is divided into National Curriculum topics (for example, Addition and subtraction, Fractions and so on). Find out what your child is doing in school and dip into the relevant practice activities as required. The index at the back of the book will help you to identify appropriate topics.

- Share the activities and support your child if necessary using the helpful quick tips at the top of most pages.

- Keep the working time short and come back to an activity if your child finds it too difficult. Ask your child to note any areas of difficulty at the back of the book. Don't worry if your child does not 'get' a concept first time, as children learn at different rates and content is likely to be covered throughout the school year.

- Check your child's answers using the answers section on www.scholastic.co.uk/100practice/mathsy4 where you will also find additional interactive activities for your child to play, and some extra resources to support your child's learning (such as number grids and a times tables chart).

- Give lots of encouragement and tick off the progress chart as your child completes each chapter.

How to use the book

This tells you which topic you're working on.

This is the title of the activity.

These boxes will help you with the activity.
(If there's not one on your page, go back and find the last one.)

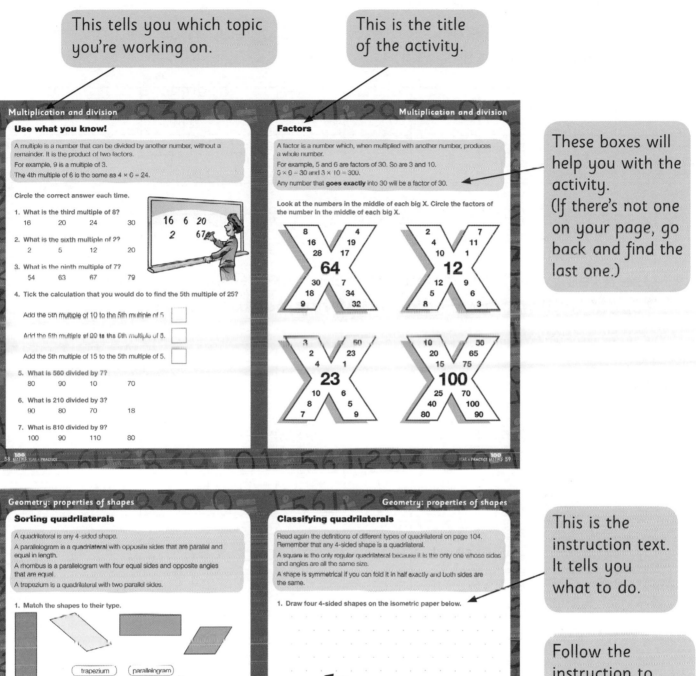

This is the instruction text. It tells you what to do.

Follow the instruction to complete the activity.

You might have to write on lines, in boxes, draw or circle things.

If you need help, ask an adult!

Counting in 6s, 7s and 9s

Counting in steps of different size helps us to understand number patterns and prepares us for work on times tables.

1	2	3	4	5	6	7	8	9	10
11	**12**	13	14	15	16	17	**18**	19	20

6, 12 and 18 are all in the 6s pattern. They are all multiples of 6.

1. **Use a red pencil. Start at 0 and count on 6. Colour the number. Repeat until you have coloured 12 numbers.**

0	1	2	3	4	5	6	7	8	9
10	11	12	13	14	15	16	17	18	19
20	21	22	23	24	25	26	27	28	29
30	31	32	33	34	35	36	37	38	39
40	41	42	43	44	45	46	47	48	49
50	51	52	53	54	55	56	57	58	59
60	61	62	63	64	65	66	67	68	69
70	71	72	73	74	75	76	77	78	79
80	81	82	83	84	85	86	87	88	89
90	91	92	93	94	95	96	97	98	99

a. What is 6 more than:

18 24   30 36   42 48

b. What is 6 less than:

12 6   42 36   60 54

c. Which numbers in the 6-times table are also multiples of 3?

all of them

2. **Now use a blue pencil. Start at 0 and count on 7. Colour the number. Count on in steps of 7, until you have coloured 12 numbers.**

a. What is 7 more than:

21 28   49 56   63 70

b. What is 7 less than:

42 35   84 77   35 28

3. **Now use a yellow pencil. Start at 0 and count on 9. Colour the number. Count on in steps of 9 until you have coloured 11 numbers.**

a. What will the 12th number be? 108

b. What is 9 more than:

18 27   36 45   63 72

c. What is 9 less than:

54 45   81 72   63 54

Counting in 25s and 50s

To count in 25s from 0 just remember these numbers: 25, 50, 75, 100.

Beyond 100, just put the 100s number in front: 125, 150, 175, 200, 225, 250, 275, 300 and so on.

Counting in 50s is just like counting in 5s: 50, 100, 150, 200, 250, 300.

1. **Finish each sequence by counting in 25s.**

   a. 75   100   *125*   150   *175*   200   *225*

   b. 925   *900*   875   *850*   825   800   *775*

   c. 41   66   *91*   116   141   *166*   191   *216*

2. **I add 25g. What is the mass now?**

   375

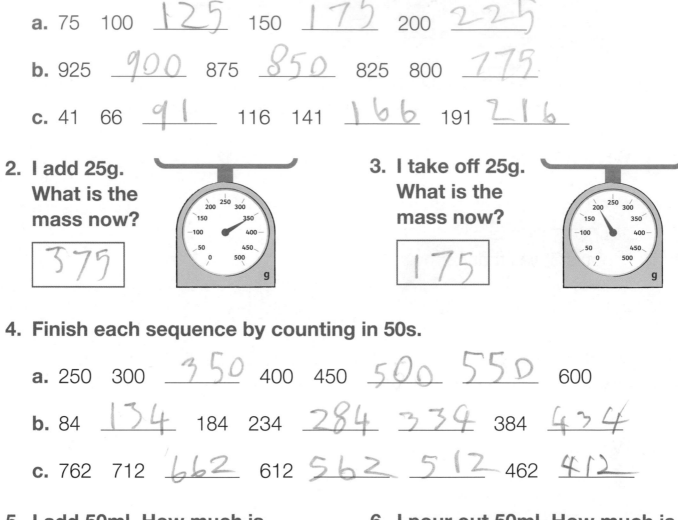

3. **I take off 25g. What is the mass now?**

   175

4. **Finish each sequence by counting in 50s.**

   a. 250   300   *350*   400   450   *500*   *550*   600

   b. 84   *134*   184   234   *284*   *334*   384   *434*

   c. 762   712   *662*   612   *562*   *512*   462   *412*

5. **I add 50ml. How much is in the jug now?**

   325

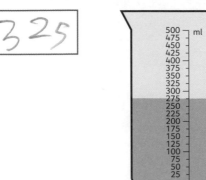

6. **I pour out 50ml. How much is in the jug now?**

   225

Counting in 1000s

To count in thousands from any 2- or 3-digit number, just put the 1000s digit in the 1000s place and then count on; only the 1000s number changes: 25, 1025, 2025, 3025, 4025.

1. Count in 1000s to fill in the missing numbers.

623	1623	2623	3623	1623	5623	6623
9578	8578	7578	6578	5578	4578	3578

2. Use counting in 1000s to work out the answers.

a. 6832 + 1000 = 7832

b. 7026 + 1000 = 8026

c. three thousand four hundred and eighty-one + 2000 = 5481

d. five thousand two hundred and seven + 3000 = 8207

e. 1000 less than 4803 = 3803

f. 1000 less than 1345 = 345

3. How far will each cyclist go if they each do 1km more?

Tip: 1000m = 1km

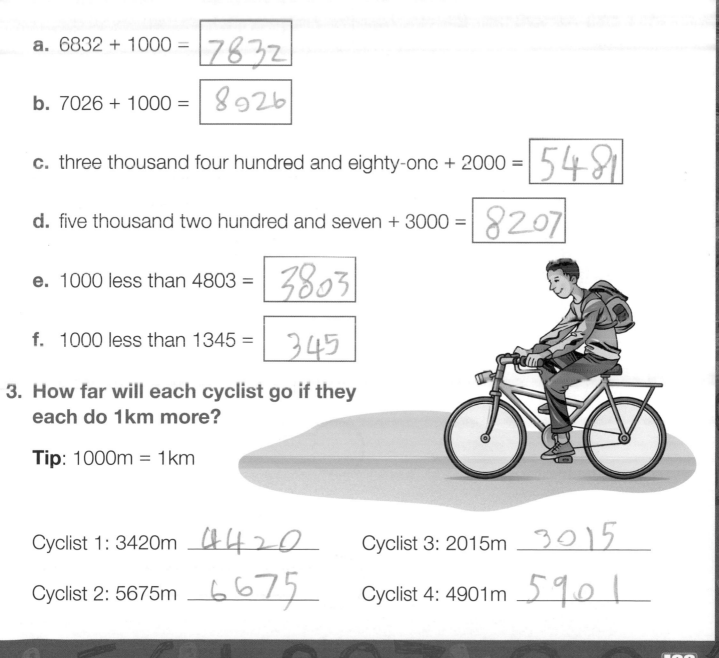

Cyclist 1: 3420m   4420

Cyclist 3: 2015m   3015

Cyclist 2: 5675m   6675

Cyclist 4: 4901m   5901

Counting with negative numbers

Practise counting on and back from 0 to 20.

Now start at 0 and count backwards, using negative numbers: 0, −1, −2, −3, −4, −5, −6 and so on. Negative numbers are used when reading temperatures: 0 = freezing; −6 is colder than −1 and −6 is less than −1.

1. Complete these sequences.

a.

48	40	32	24	16	8	0	−8	−16

b.

−16	−12	−8	−4	0	4	8	12	16

c.

35	28	21	14	7	0	−7	−14	−21

2. Fill in the missing numbers on these thermometers.

a.

−2

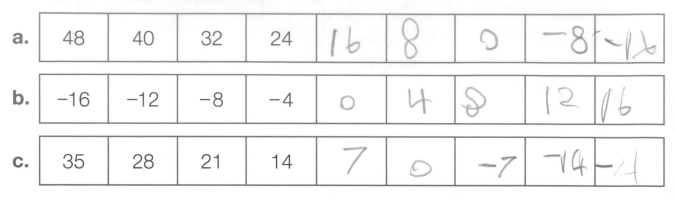

b.

−6

c.

20

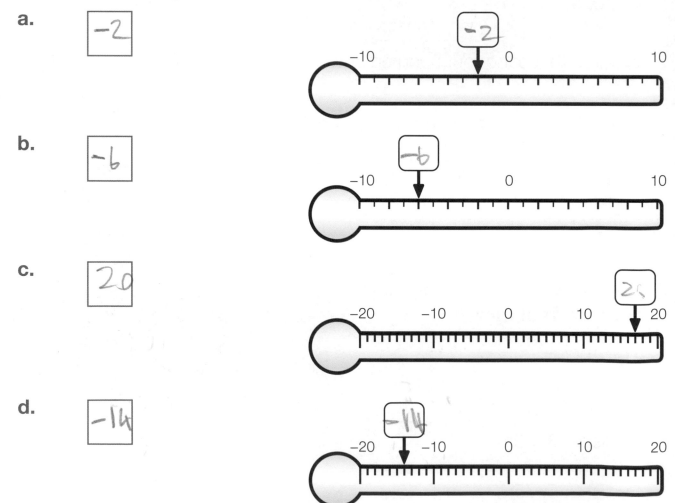

d.

−14

4-digit place value

The position of a number changes its value. Larger numbers need a large number in the 1000s place; smaller numbers need a small number in the 1000s place.

1. **Alex has four number cards: 5, 8, 2 and 7.**

   a. What is the largest number he can make using all four cards?

   _8752_

   b. What is the smallest?

   _2578_

2. **Now do the same for these numbers.**

   a. 9 3 4 1: largest _9431_ smallest _1349_

   b. 5 6 5 2: largest _6552_ smallest _2556_

   c. 9 9 8 8   largest _9988_ smallest _8899_

   d. 3 0 6 0   largest _6300_ smallest _63_

Number and place value

Partitioning 4-digit numbers

4-digit numbers can be partitioned into 1000s, 100s, 10s and 1s.

So, 4567 =

1000s	100s	10s	1s
4	5	6	7

= 4000 + 500 + 60 + 7.

1. **Write the correct numbers in the spaces.**

   a. 1234 = 1000 + 200 + 30 + __4__

   b. __8765__ = 8000 + 700 + 60 + 5

   c. 2659 = __2000__ + 600 + 50 + 9

   d. 6000 + 700 + __20__ + 1 = 6721

   e. 9583 = 9000 + __500__ + 80 + 3

   f. 3724 = 700 + 4 + 20 + __3000__

   g. 1562 = 1000 + __2__ + 500 + 60

   h. __6499__ = 9 + 6000 + 90 + 400

   i. __5252__ = 50 + 5000 + 200 + 2

   j. 3527 = __500__ + __7__ + __20__ + __3000__

   k. 6074 = __6000__ + __70__ + __0__ + __4__

   l. 3003 = __0__ + __0__ + __3__ + __3000__

3724

9583

1562

Ordering numbers

When ordering 4-digit numbers, first look at the 1000s digit; then the 100s, then the 10s and then the 1s.

For example, look at 4672 and 6742. 6742 has the biggest 1000s number, so it is the biggest number.

1. **Answer the following questions by writing 'Yes' or 'No' below.**

   a. Is 1265 more than 1562? __No__

   b. Is 29 + 21 equal to 76 − 26? __Yes__

   c. Is 3003 fewer than 3030? __Yes__

   d. Is 7025 more than 7250? __No__

   e. Is 5252 smaller than 5225? __No__

   f. Is 6074 larger than 6047? __Yes__

2. **Fill in the boxes with the correct sign, < (less than) or > (greater than), so that these number sentences make sense. The first one has been done for you.**

   a. 1654 > 1546

   b. 201 < 210

   c. −10 > −12

   d. 9242 < 9422

3. **Arrange these numbers in order of size, starting with the largest.**

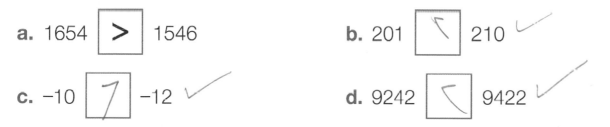

   6789   7896   8967   6978   6987   9876   7898

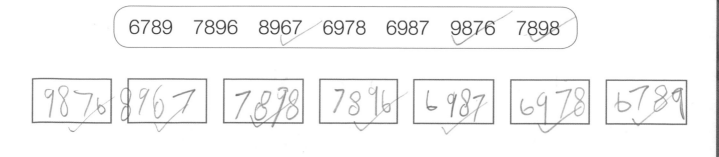

9876   8967   7898   7896   6987   6978   6789

Ordering amounts

Ordering amounts is just like ordering numbers.

Which is heaviest, 4567kg or 4675kg? They both have four 1000s so you need to look at the 100s. **600** is more than **500**; so 4675kg is the heaviest.

Now consider 0.**85**kg and 0.**65**kg. Look at the tenths first. 0.**8**5 has more tenths than 0.**6**5, so it is heavier.

1. **Fill in the boxes with the correct sign, < or >, so that these number sentences make sense.**

   a. 0.25kg [<] 0.36kg ✓   b. 1.30kg [>] 1.04kg ✓

   c. 0.05kg [<] 0.50kg ✓   d. 3.72kg [>] 2.27kg ✓

2. **Write down the answers to these problems.**

   a. Which is heavier: 3725kg or 3527kg? ___3725kg___ ✓

   b. Which is lighter: 8020g or 8002g? ___8002g___ ✓

   c. Write a mass that is greater than 6999kg. ___7000kg___ ✓

3. **Arrange these amounts in order of size, starting with the largest.**

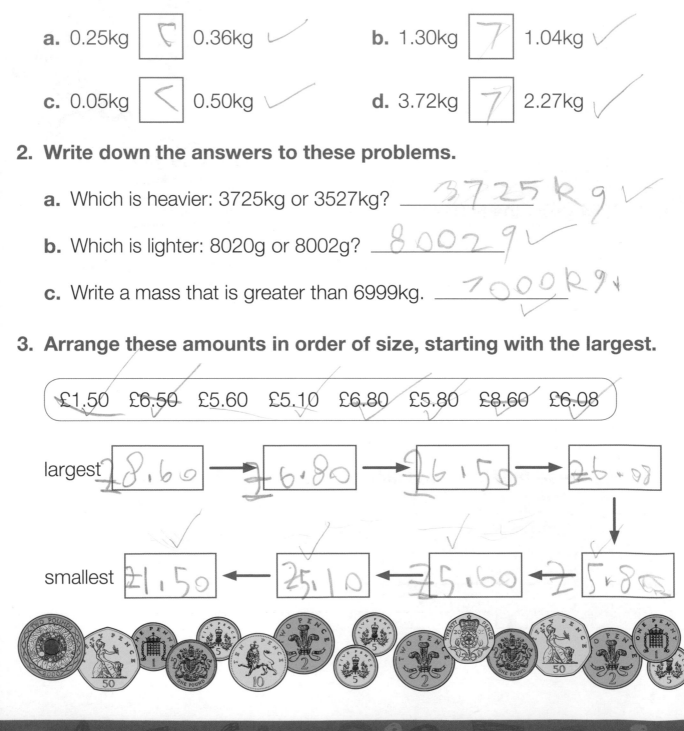

£1.50   £6.50   £5.60   £5.10   £6.80   £5.80   £8.60   £6.08

largest [£8.60] → [£6.80] → [£6.50] → [£6.08]

smallest [£1.50] ← [£5.10] ← [£5.60] ← [£5.80]

Numbers in numerals and words

Practise writing all 1-digit numbers in words. Practise writing all multiples of 10 in words. Remember:

100 = hundred; 1000 = thousand; so 2064 = two thousand and sixty-four.

1. Write these amounts in figures.

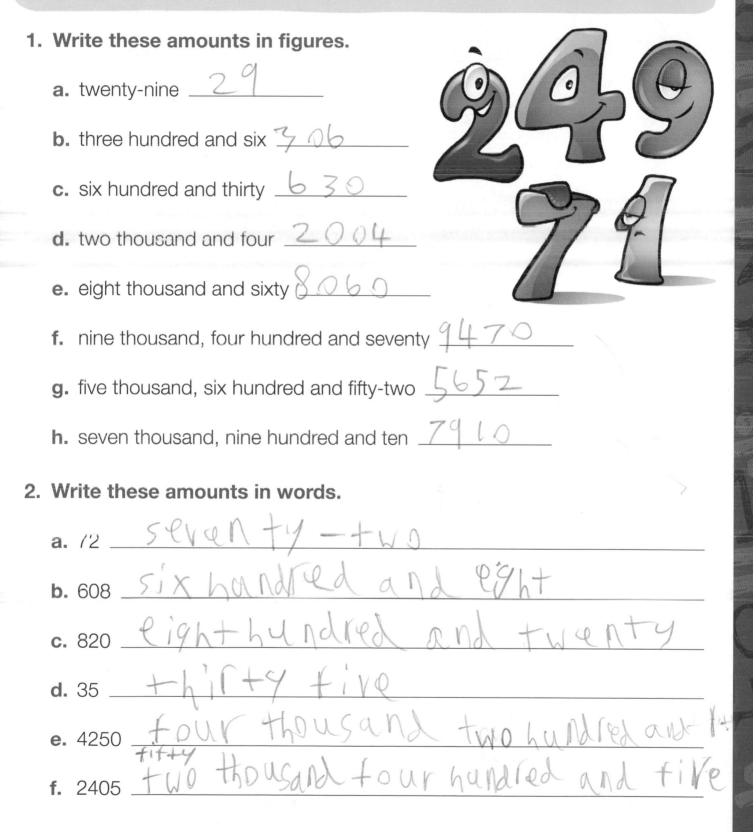

a. twenty-nine ___29___

b. three hundred and six ___306___

c. six hundred and thirty ___630___

d. two thousand and four ___2004___

e. eight thousand and sixty ___8060___

f. nine thousand, four hundred and seventy ___9470___

g. five thousand, six hundred and fifty-two ___5652___

h. seven thousand, nine hundred and ten ___7910___

2. Write these amounts in words.

a. 72 ___seventy-two___

b. 608 ___six hundred and eight___

c. 820 ___eight hundred and twenty___

d. 35 ___thirty five___

e. 4250 ___four thousand two hundred and fifty___

f. 2405 ___two thousand four hundred and five___

Roman numerals

The Romans used only 7 letters to make numbers. There is no letter for 0.

I	V	X	L	C	D	M
1	5	10	50	100	500	1000

You combine letters to make numbers, such as VI = 6 (5 and 1) and LXVI = 66 (50 and 10, and 5 and 1).

The numbers 4, 9, 40, 90, 400 and 900 are written as subtractions. For example; IV = 4 (5 – 1) with the I before the V to signify one less than that number.

$$9 = IX \ (10 - 1) \quad 40 = XL \ (50 - 10) \quad 90 = XC \ (100 - 10)$$
$$400 = CD \ (500 - 100) \quad 900 = CM \ (1000 - 100)$$

1. Write the Roman numerals for:

a. 2 [ ]   **b.** 7 [ ]   **c.** 19 [ ]

d. 11 [ ]   **e.** 22 [ ]   **f.** 52 [ ]

g. 49 [ ]   **h.** 101 [ ]

2. Fill in the missing Roman numerals on the clock.

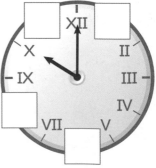

3. Write your answers using Roman numerals.

a. VI + II = [ ]   **b.** IV + VI = [ ]

c. XXX + XX = [ ]   **d.** C – X = [ ]

e. L + VIII = [ ]   **f.** XLII + XII = [ ]

4. Match each number with the correct Roman numeral.

4	XII
6	XXV
12	CVII
18	XC
25	VI
90	XVIII
107	IV

5. Add Roman numerals to complete these number sentences. The first one has been done for you.

a. 5 = [IV] + [I]   b. 10 = [ ] + [ ]

c. 50 = [ ] + [ ]   d. 100 = [ ] + [ ]

e. 500 = [ ] + [ ]   f. 1000 = [ ] + [ ]

6. Choose the correct word for each sentence.

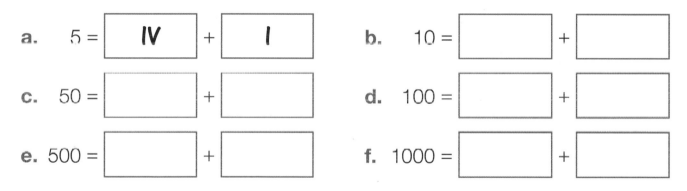

smaller   bigger   0   /

a. Roman numerals use _____ letters to make numbers.

b. There is no symbol for _____.

c. The first letter represents the _____ number.

d. Putting I before X makes it _____.

10, 100 and 1000 more or less

When you add or subtract 10, the 10s number changes.
For example, 40**9**2 − 10 = 40**8**2.

When you add or subtract 100, the 100s number changes.
For example, 4**0**92 + 100 = 4**1**92.

When you add or subtract 1000, the 1000s number changes.
For example, **4**092 − 1000 = **3**092.

1. **Add and subtract 10, 100 and 1000 from each number.**

−1000	−100	−10	Number	+10	+100	+1000
			3040			
			5395			
			7002			
			1256			
			4609			
			6048			
			8794			
			7593			

+1000   +100   +10   −10   −100   −1000

Rounding to the nearest 10

To round to the nearest 10, look at the number of 1s. If there are 5 or more, round up to the next 10. If there are less than 5, round down to the 10 before.

So for 67**3**, **3** is less than 5, so round down: 670.
For 67**8**, **8** is greater than 5, so round up: 680.

1. **Round these distances to the nearest 10 kilometres.**

   a. 134km _130 KM_

   b. 655km _660 KM_

   c. 4009km _4010 KM_

   d. 827km _830 KM_

   e. 291km _290 KM_

   f. 3913km _3910 KM_
      _3910 km_

2. **Round these distances from London to the nearest 10 miles.**

Town	Distance	Nearest 10 miles
York	209 miles	210 miles
Norwich	115 miles	120 miles
Leeds	196 miles	200 miles
Cardiff	155 miles	160 miles
Brighton	53 miles	50 Miles
Glasgow	405 miles	410 miles
New York	3462 miles	3460

3. **Write a number between 0 and 100. It must be nearer to 100 than 0. Place it on the number line.**

   0 _50_ 100

Rounding to the nearest 100 and 1000

To round to the nearest 100, look at the 10s digit.

To round to nearest 1000 look at the 100s digit.

Is it 5 or more? Round up. Is it less than 5? Round down.

For example, for 3**6**3: round up to 400. For 4**3**63: round down to 4000.

1. **Use the digits to make six 4-digit numbers. Then complete the chart.**

3   4   5   6

My 4-digit number	Round to nearest 100	Round to nearest 1000
6543	6400	7000
3456	3500	2000
6453	6500	5000
5634	5500	6000
3564	3600	4000
4635	4500	5000

2. **Bill went to see his local football team play. The local newspaper reported that 3200 people were at the game. This figure was rounded to the nearest 100.**

   a. What was the highest number of people that could have been at the game? 3399

   b. What was the lowest number? 3201

   c. What is this lowest number, rounded to the nearest 1000? 3000

Rounding to the nearest 10, 100 or 1000

Remember, to round to the nearest 10, look at the 1s digit.

To round to the nearest 100 look, at the 10s digit.

To round to the nearest 1000, look at the 100s digit.

1. Round these lengths to the nearest 10cm.

a. 722cm ___720___

b. 357cm ___360___

c. 1045cm ___1050___

d. 2664cm ___2660___

2. Round these capacities to the nearest 100ml.

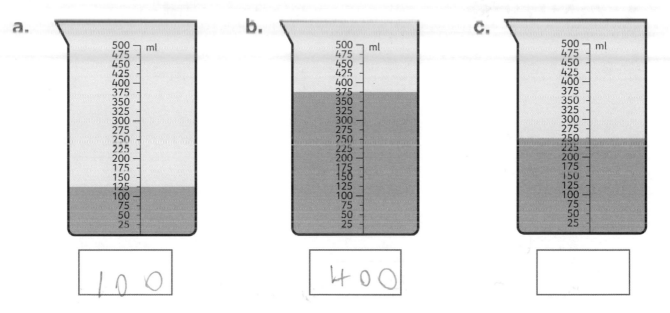

a. ___100___

b. ___400___

c. _____

3. Round these river lengths to complete the chart.

Name	Length (km)	Nearest 10km	Nearest 100km	Nearest 1000km
Amazon	6516	6520	6500	7000
Zaire	4373	4370	4400	4000
Lena	4256	4260	4300	4000
Nile	6669	6670	6750	7000

Estimating and approximating

To estimate calculations, round the numbers up or down to the nearest 1, 10, 100 or 1000. For example, 56 + 73, 60 (round up) + 70 (round down) = 130. The estimated answer = 130. The actual answer is 56 + 73 = 129.

1. From the list, pick the amount that you think will be nearest to the actual answer of the problem and write it in the first box. Then write the correct answer in the second box.

650   200   3000   20   400   500

a. 32cm – 14cm = ☐ ☐   b. 659ml + 21ml = ☐ ☐

c. £247 – £35 = ☐ ☐   d. 89m + 407m = ☐ ☐

e. 460m – 63m = ☐ ☐   f. 239g + 3001g = ☐ ☐

2. Estimate the numbers marked by the arrows on the number line.

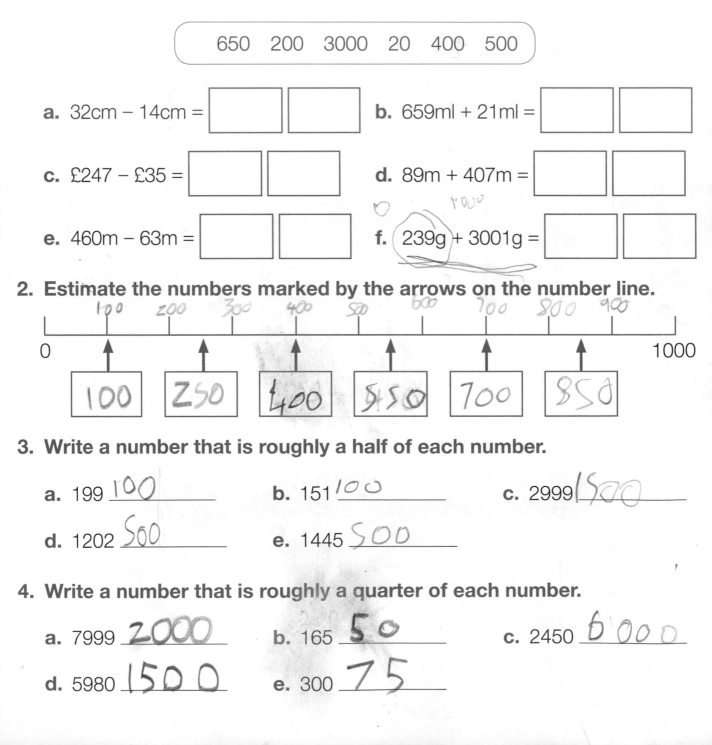

| 100 | 250 | 400 | 550 | 700 | 850 |

3. Write a number that is roughly a half of each number.

a. 199 _100_   b. 151 _100_   c. 2999 _1500_

d. 1202 _500_   e. 1445 _500_

4. Write a number that is roughly a quarter of each number.

a. 7999 _2000_   b. 165 _50_   c. 2450 _6000_

d. 5980 _1500_   e. 300 _75_

Place-value test

To order numbers, compare the 1000s digit first, the 100s second, the 10s third and finally the 1s.

Larger numbers have the largest 1000s numbers. For example, **4**560 is greater than **3**560.

46**7**2 is bigger than 43**7**2 because the 100s number is bigger.

1. **Fill in the missing amounts in these sequences.**

   a. £2.28 _£2.21_ _£2.14_ £2.07 £2.00 _£1.93_

   b. 345g 395g _445g_ _495g_ _545g_ 595g

   c. _6025_ 5725 5125 _5125_ 4825 _4525_

2. **Now count back in 4s from 95 to 55.**

   95 | 91 | 87 | 83 | 79 | 75 | 71 | 67 | 63 | 59 | 55

   If you went below 55; would 35 be in your sequence?   (Yes) / No

3. **Read and answer these questions carefully.**

   a. How many 1s are there in two thousand and forty-nine? _9_

   b. What does the digit 7 stand for in 3726? _700_

   c. Write down in numerals the number five thousand, four hundred and eight. _5408_

4. **Arrange these numbers in order of size, starting with the largest.**

   7439   3140   3041   7394   7934   3104   7943   8506

   | 8506 | 7943 | 7934 | 7439 | 7394 | 3140 | 3104 | 3041 |

Adding and subtracting mentally (1)

To add or subtract several numbers mentally, look for pairs of numbers that total 10, look for near 10s and look for doubles.

For example, to add 8 + 6 + 2 + 5. 8 + 2 = 10; 6 + 5 is a near double (calculate 12 − 1). So 10 + 11 = 21.

Work out these problems in your head using the methods above.

- Can you make pairs of numbers that can help you?
- Can you round the numbers to the nearest 10 to help you?
- Can you find doubles or near-doubles?

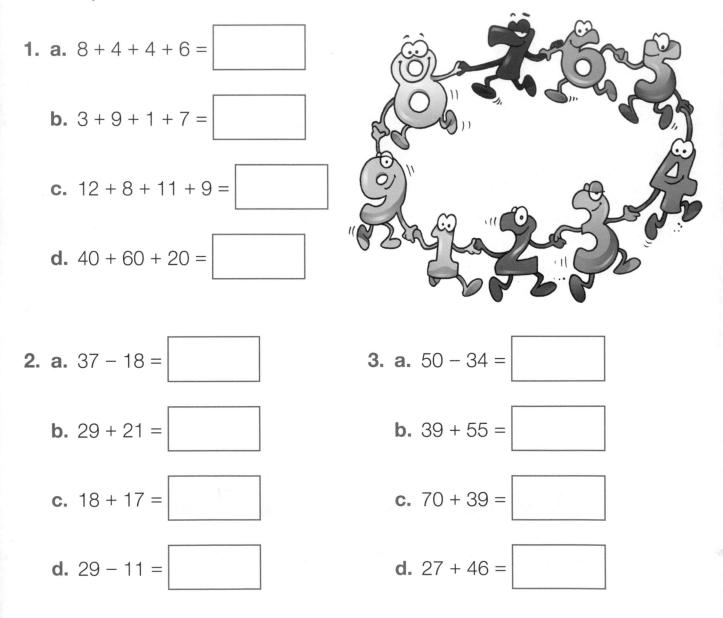

1. a. 8 + 4 + 4 + 6 =

b. 3 + 9 + 1 + 7 =

c. 12 + 8 + 11 + 9 =

d. 40 + 60 + 20 =

2. a. 37 − 18 =

b. 29 + 21 =

c. 18 + 17 =

d. 29 − 11 =

3. a. 50 − 34 =

b. 39 + 55 =

c. 70 + 39 =

d. 27 + 46 =

Adding and subtracting mentally (2)

Using the doubles, multiples of 10 and partitioning numbers can help with mental addition and subtraction. For example:

23 + 8 + 17 + 6 can be partitioned to: 23 + 7 + 10 = 40 and 8 + 6 = 14
so 40 + 14 = 54

Work out these problems in your head using the methods above.

- Can you make pairs of numbers that can help you?
- Can you round the numbers to the nearest multiple of 10 to help you?
- Can you partition the numbers to help you?

1. a. 7 + 14 + 5 + 26 = ☐   **2. a.** 85 – 28 – ☐

b. 34 + 9 + 6 + 11 = ☐   **b.** 88 + 41 = ☐

c. 48 + 12 + 7 + 35 = ☐   **c.** 99 + 88 = ☐

d. 90 + 110 + 60 = ☐   **d.** 77 – 49 = ☐

3. a. 184 – 62 = ☐

b. 69 + 47 – ☐

c. 180 – 52 = ☐

d. 87 + 66 = ☐

Adding and subtracting 2-digit numbers mentally

Start with the larger number. Add or subtract the 10s.
Then add or subtract the 1s.

So, for 32 + 57 start with the larger number (57) then add on the 10s (30) then add on the 1s (2). 57 + 30 = 87 + 2 = 89.

1. **Answer these questions in your head.**

   a. 45 + 52 =

   b. 56 + 27 =

   c. 65 – 42 =

   d. 43 – 27 =

   e. 17 + 81 =

   f. 19 + 74 =

   g. 34 – 24 =

   h. 78 – 64 =

2. **What number do I add to 38 to make 56?**

3. **Write down how you would add 19 to 67.**

   _____

4. **How do I know that 94 – 21 could not be 74?**

   _____

5. **A pair of numbers has a difference of 15. What could these numbers be?**

   _____

Adding and subtracting multiples of 10 and 100

Think of your addition and subtraction bonds to 20.

You know $5 + 7 = 12$, so 50 (five 10s) + 70 (seven 10s) = 120 (twelve 10s).
You can also work out that $500 + 700 = 1200$ (twelve 100s).

1. Read each question. Use jottings to work it out. Write the answer.
   Now write another calculation to check that the answer is correct.

Question	Jottings	Answer	Check
70 + 60			
70 + 90			
100 – 60			
120 – 70			
500 + 400			
700 – 600			

Adding and subtracting multiples of 10, 100 and 1000

Think of your addition and subtraction bonds to 20.

You know 12 − 8 = 4. So 120 − 80 = 40 and 1200 (twelve 100s) − 800 (eight 100s) = 400 (four 100s).

Use what you know to help you work out what you don't know!

1. Read each question. Use jottings to work it out. Write the answer. Now write another calculation to check that the answer is correct.

Question	Jottings	Answer	Check
40 + 90			
120 − 50			
800 + 400			
900 − 700			
3000 + 6000			
5000 − 2000			

Choose the best strategy to add and subtract

Remember all the different strategies you can use to add and subtract: pairs to 10, near 10s, doubles, near doubles, largest number first, partitioning numbers and rounding numbers.

1. **Work out these additions and subtractions in your head, using the best strategy.**

   a. 23 + 17 = _____

   b. 80 − 12 = _____

   c. 29 + 11 = _____

   d. 30 − 18 = _____

   e. 47 − 18 = _____

   f. 12 + 78 = _____

   g. 100 − 34 = _____

   h. 49 + 11 = _____

   i. 17 + 4 = _____

   j. 29 − 8 = _____

   k. 49 + 48 = _____

   l. 64 + 36 = _____

   m. 101 + 57 = _____

   n. 56 + 57 = _____

   o. 119 − 31 = _____

Written strategies for adding

To add horizontally, first add the 1s mentally, then add the 10s mentally.
Finally add the 1s and 10s totals mentally. So $27 + 65 = 12 + 80 = 92$.

To add using columns, write the sum vertically like this:

```
   6 5
+  2 7
```
1 2 (First add the 1s (5 + 7 = 12)
8 0 Then add the 10s (60 + 20 = 80)
9 2 Then add to find the total (12 + 80 = 92)

1. Do these sums two ways.

- Work horizontally and show your workings.

- Write the sum vertically. Show your workings.

The first one has been done for you.

$37 + 63 = 10 + 90 = 100$

```
   37
+  63
   10
   90
  100
```

a. 65 + 45 =

b. 83 + 89 =

c. 123 + 45 =

d. 246 + 78 =

Column skills: addition

To add using columns:

```
  3 7 5
+   5 8
─────────
  4 3 3
  1 1
```

Add the 1s column first. Put any 10s below the 10s column to add later.

Add the 10s, including 10s carried from the 1s column. Put any 100s under the 100s column to add later.

Add the 100s, including any 100s carried from the 10s column.

1. **Look at the additions below. Work out the total of the two numbers using the column method. The first one has been done for you.**

	1	4	5	
+		8	9	
	2	**3**	**4**	
	1	1		

a.

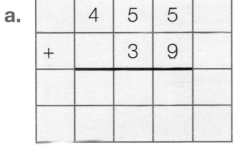

	4	5	5	
+		3	9	

b.

	5	7	7	
+		9	9	

c.

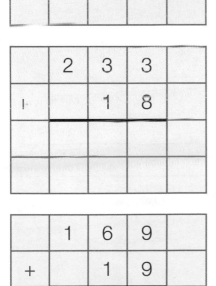

	2	3	3	
+		1	8	

d.

	6	8	9	
+		2	7	

e.

	1	6	9	
+		1	9	

f.

	8	9	4	
+		2	8	

Written strategies for subtracting

You can partition numbers to make subtraction easier.

Here is an example:

$$345 \quad {}^{200}\,\cancel{300} \quad \text{and} \quad {}^{130}\,\cancel{40} \quad \text{and} \quad {}^{1}5$$
$$-\underline{\ 76\ } \qquad\qquad\qquad\qquad 70 \quad \text{and} \quad 6$$
$$\underline{200 \quad \text{and} \quad 60 \quad \text{and} \quad 9} = \underline{269}$$

First work out the 1s, then the 10s, then the 100s.
You may need to exchange 10s or 100s.

1. Practice subtracting numbers using partitioning.

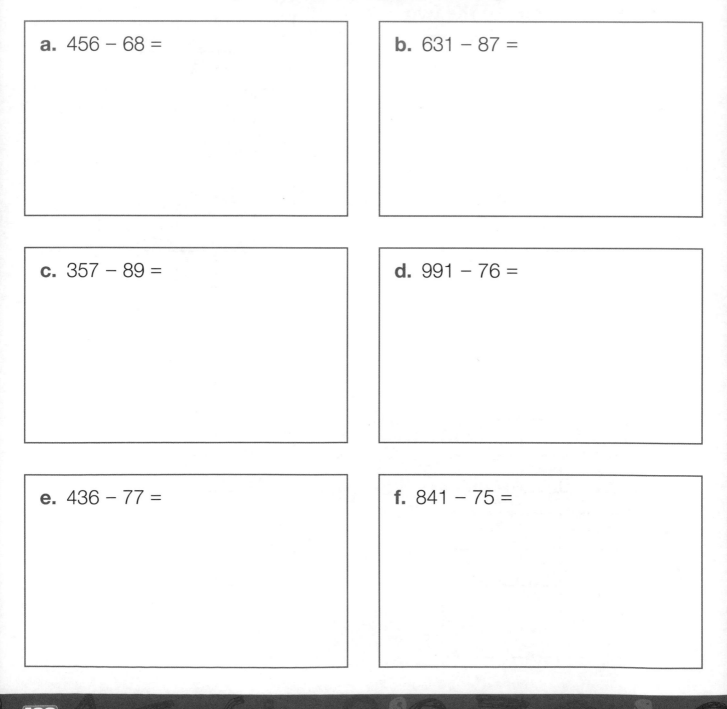

a. 456 – 68 =	**b.** 631 – 87 =
c. 357 – 89 =	**d.** 991 – 76 =
e. 436 – 77 =	**f.** 841 – 75 =

Column skills: subtraction

To subtract using columns:

$$
\begin{array}{r}
{\scriptstyle 1 \;\; 13\;\; 1}\\
2\cancel{4}6\\
-\;\;\;68\\
\hline
178
\end{array}
$$

Subtract the 1s first. For 6 – 8 we need to exchange a 10.
1s become: 16 – 8 = 8. Write 8 in the 1s column.

Subtract the 10s. For 30 – 60 we need to exchange a 100.
10s become: 130 – 60 = 70. Write 7 in the 10s column.

Subtract the 100s. 100 – 0 = 100. Write 1 in the 100s column.

1. **Look at the subtractions below. Using the space provided, set out and work out the answers to the subtraction questions using the column method.**

a. 145 – 89

b. 233 – 14

c. 168 – 19

d. 577 – 98

e. 684 – 27

f. 894 – 28

Adding larger numbers

To add larger numbers using columns:

```
  3 4 2 7
    5 8 1
+     6 5
  4 0 7 3
  1  1  1
```

Add the 1s: 13. Write 3 in the 1s column and one 10 under the 10s column.

Add the 10s: 170. Write 7 in the 10s column and one 100 under the 100s column.

Add the 100s: 1000. Write 0 in the 100s column and one 1000 under the 1000s column.

Add the 1000s: 4000. Write 4 in the 1000s column.

1. **Choose one number from each column. Add them together. Show your working out in the box below. Do this three more times.**

1032	261	75
4929	564	63
6306	385	49
3704	832	27

Subtracting larger numbers

To subtract large numbers using columns:

Subtract the 1s. For 3 – 4 we need to exchange a 10.
1s become: 13 – 4 = 9. Write 9 in the 1s column.

Subtract the 10s. For 60 – 90 we need to exchange a 100.
10s become: 160 – 90 = 70. Write 7 in the 10s column.

Subtract the 100s. For 100 – 400 we need to exchange a
1000. 100s become: 1100 – 400 = 700.
Write 7 in the 100s column.

Subtract the 1000s. 2000 – 0. Write 2 in the 1000s column.

1. **Choose one number from each set . Use them to create a
subtraction. Use the column method to work out the answers.
Do this three more times.**

Set 1

786	495
1048	873

Set 2

633	292
189	376

Addition and subtraction practice (1)

Line up your columns carefully.
Remember: if you exchange a 10, 100 or 1000, you must also reduce the column you have exchanged it from.

1. **Use the boxes to show your working out and answers.**

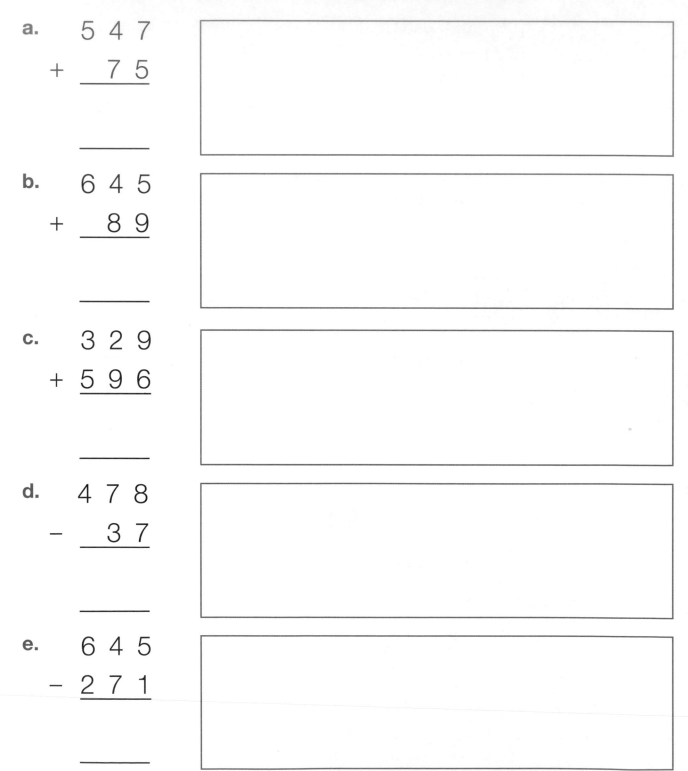

a.
```
   5 4 7
+    7 5
_____
```

b.
```
   6 4 5
+    8 9
_____
```

c.
```
   3 2 9
+ 5 9 6
_____
```

d.
```
   4 7 8
–    3 7
_____
```

e.
```
   6 4 5
– 2 7 1
_____
```

Addition and subtraction practice (2)

Remember: if a column adds up to 10 or more, you must put the 1 under the column to the left, so that it can be added on to that column's total.

1. Use the boxes to show your working out and answers.

a.
```
   3 7 2 9
+    3 4 3
─────────
```

b.
```
   4 6 3 8
+  1 3 6 1
─────────
```

c.
```
   5 7 2 6
+  2 4 1 5
─────────
```

d.
```
   2 7 4 8
-    1 6 9
─────────
```

e.
```
   7 3 5 9
－ 2 4 8 2
─────────
```

Estimate and check (1)

To estimate the answer to an addition, you can round both numbers to the nearest 10. Remember: if the 1s are 5 or more, round up; if they are less than 5, round down.

For example, for 36 round up to 40. For 34 round down to 30.

1. Read each question. Use rounding to estimate each sum.

2. Add the numbers mentally to find the actual total.

3. Now write another calculation to check your total is correct.

Question	Estimate of sum	Actual total	Check
18 + 29			
25 + 71			
43 + 78			
92 + 54			
94 + 95			
67 + 84			

Estimate and check (2)

Subtraction is the opposite of addition. It is the inverse operation. We use the inverse operation to check if our calculations are correct. So: 12 + **4** = 16. 16 − 12 = **4**. The numbers in both calculations must be the same.

1. In the second column, write an addition or subtraction number sentence using the two numbers in the first column. Do not write the answer yet.

2. Round each number and estimate the answer to the calculation. Write this in the third column.

3. Check your estimate using an inverse operation. Write this in the fourth column.

4. Now write the actual answer next to the number sentence.

Numbers	Number sentence and answer	Estimate using rounding	Check using an inverse operation
36, 23	36 + 23 = 59	40 + 20 = 60	60 − 40 = 20
47, 48			
38, 73			
85, 97			
118, 83			
121, 78			
134, 35			
127, 44			
168, 23			
155, 48			
99, 98			

Adding money using columns

You can use column addition to add money. It is the same as adding larger numbers. You must keep your columns lined up and make sure the decimal point is always lined up. Start by adding the 1s in the pence first, and work out each column, moving left.

1. Choose any five pairs of these six amounts of money to add. Set out your work using the squared paper below and be sure to keep your decimal points underneath each other. One has been done for you.

£13.56   £8.76   £6.78   £3.14   £2.99   £8.12

```
    £ 8 . 7 6
  + £ 6 . 7 8
  £ 1 5 . 5 4
        1     1
```

Subtracting money using columns

You can use column subtraction to add money. It is the same as subtracting larger numbers. You must keep your columns lined up and make sure the decimal point is always lined up. Start by subtracting the 1s in the pence first, and work out each column, moving left.

1. Choose any five pairs of these six amounts of money to subtract. Set out your work using the squared paper below and be sure to keep your decimal points underneath each other. One has been done for you.

£13.56   £8.76   £6.78   £3.14   £2.99   £8.12

		£	⁷8̶	.	¹⁶7̶	¹6
-		£	6	.	7	8
		£	1	.	9	8

Addition and subtraction money problems (1)

Read each problem. Decide whether it is an addition or subtraction problem. Write the numbers for the calculation in columns, and then work through each column to find the answer.

1. **Jamie has been saving his pocket money and has decided to go shopping. Help him decide how to spend it.**

a. How much would it cost Jamie to buy the magazine and the model?

_____

b. What is the difference in price between the DVD and the PC game?

_____

c. What is the cost of the DVD and the CD?

_____

d. Jamie decides to buy the model and a magazine and still has £2.55 change. How much did he have to spend altogether?

_____

Addition and subtraction money problems (2)

Read each question and decide which calculation you need to do. Decide which numbers you need in your calculation. Some questions may need more than one calculation.

1. These are the prices of some vegetables.

   Cauliflower £0.90   Potatoes £1.25 per 2.5kg   Carrots £0.60 per kg

   a. I buy one cauliflower, 5kg potatoes and 1kg carrots.
   How much have I spent?

   _____

   b. I have £5. I buy two cauliflowers, 2.5kg potatoes and $\frac{1}{2}$ kg carrots.
   How much change do I get?

   _____

2. Jack wants to buy some plants. He buys one tray of plants for £2.50 and one for £3.25. How much change does he get from £10?

   _____

3. Find the total cost of each of these shop transactions A, B and C.

   a.   £ 6 . 5 0   b.   9 9 p   c.   £ 9 . 9 5
       + £ 1 2 . 0 0   + 7 6 p   + £ 0 . 8 8
       _____   _____   _____

       _____   _____   _____

4. For each of the transactions above, work out the change received by the customer.

   a. Customer A pays with £20. _____

   b. Customer B pays with £5. _____

   c. Customer C pays with £15. _____

Magical measures problems

1. **Make a spell to cure the wizard's cold. The spell must weigh no more than 1 kilogram. You must use at least three different objects. You may use as many of each object as you wish.**

Tip: You may need to try several solutions, before finding one that works. There may be more than one correct answer!

1 slice slippery snake 125g

4 shiny conkers 250g

5 hairy spiders 75g

3 spiky crocodile toes 350g

10 wriggly worms 125g

2 soft squirrel tails 50g

1 cup stinging nettles 350g

6 cactus leaves 250g

My spell

_____

_____

_____

_____

Measures problems (+ and –)

Read each problem and decide if it is an addition or subtraction problem.

Write the addition or subtraction sentence and decide whether you can solve it mentally or if you need to do a written calculation. Write the answers.

1. Jack walked 540m and Jill walked 367m. How far did they walk altogether?

_____

_____

2. A rectangle has one side which is 34cm and another side which is 21cm. What is its perimeter?

_____

_____

3. A piece of ribbon is 12.34m and another piece is 3.67m. What is the total length of the pieces of ribbon?

_____

_____

4. Amy is 108cm tall and Emma is 132cm. What is the difference between their heights?

_____

_____

Money and measures problems (+ and −)

Look at each word problem and decide if you need to do an addition or a subtraction.

Write the correct addition or subtraction sentence, then solve the problem.

1. Imran has saved £6.86. He is given another £3.84 in pocket money. How much does he now have altogether?

_____

2. Graham cycled 5.45km on a sponsored cycle. Joy cycled 3.61km. How much further did Graham cycle than Joy?

_____

3. There were 350ml of water in a measuring jug. 275ml was poured out of the jug. How much water was left in the jug?

_____

4. 123 people went to see the school play on Day 1. 120 went on Day 2. 85 went on Day 3. How many people attended altogether?

_____

5. Mr Peters had 165cm of dowel rod. He cut off 77cm of rod. How much was left?

_____

6. There are 3250 people in a football stadium watching a football match. 750 leave early. How many are left at the end of the match?

_____

Addition and subtraction challenge

Remember: **total**, **sum** and **plus** all mean **add**. **Take away** and **difference** both mean **subtract**.

Look at each problem. If it contains different units, convert each number to the same unit to make it easier. For example, if you are subtracting 35cm from 3m, change both to either cm or m: 300cm = 35cm or 3.00m = 0.35m.

1. What is the total of 124, 39 and 25?	**2.** Subtract 84 pence from £2.50.
3. Find the difference between 132 and 69.	**4.** Work out the sum of 240 and 170.
5. From 400 take away 175.	**6.** Add £2.60 to £4.35.
7. Work out the total of 111, 222 and 334.	**8.** From 2 metres, subtract 87 centimetres.
9. What is 104 plus 97?	**10.** What is 235 take away 147?

Quick recall ×2 to ×10

Practise saying the 2-, 3-, 4-, 5- and 10-times tables.
Write down any tables facts you cannot recall easily.

1. See how quickly you can complete these questions.

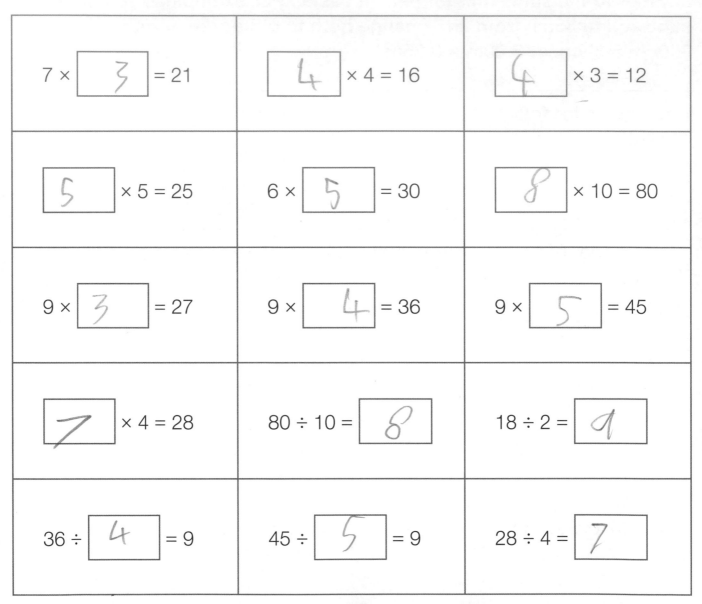

7 × ☐ 3 ☐ = 21

☐ 4 ☐ × 4 = 16

☐ 4 ☐ × 3 = 12

☐ 5 ☐ × 5 = 25

6 × ☐ 5 ☐ = 30

☐ 8 ☐ × 10 = 80

9 × ☐ 3 ☐ = 27

9 × ☐ 4 ☐ = 36

9 × ☐ 5 ☐ = 45

☐ 7 ☐ × 4 = 28

80 ÷ 10 = ☐ 8 ☐

18 ÷ 2 = ☐ 9 ☐

36 ÷ ☐ 4 ☐ = 9

45 ÷ ☐ 5 ☐ = 9

28 ÷ 4 = ☐ 7 ☐

Multiplication facts ×2 to ×10

Being able to recall multiplication facts quickly makes written multiplication much easier. Practise saying each times table, to make your recall faster.
To fill in a multiplication grid, multiply a top number by a side number.
For example, 3 × 2 = 6 and 6 × 2 = 12.

×	3	6
2	6	12

Complete the multiplication grids.

1.

×	2	10	5	1
1	2	10	5	1
4	8	40	20	4
5	10	50	25	5
3	6	30	15	3

2.

×	5	6	7	2
3	15	18	21	6
6	30	36	42	12
4	20	24	28	8
5	25	3.0	35	10

3.

×	9	4	6	10
2	18	8	12	20
7	63	28	42	70
3	27	12	18	30
8	72	32	48	80

4.

×	5	8	7	3
6	30	48	42	18
1	5	8	7	3
9	45	72	63	27
4	20	32	28	12

The 7- and 9-times tables

Practise saying each times table, to make your recall faster. You will see patterns in some of the times tables.

1. **Read each number sentence and circle the correct answer from the options in the second column.**

The 7-times table				
10 × 7	7	17	70	10
8 × 7	56	47	49	54
4 × 7	24	28	32	21
7 × 7	42	49	52	35
5 × 7	40	35	25	30
3 × 7	14	21	28	7
56 ÷ 7	7	8	4	49
21 ÷ 7	7	3	24	49
49 ÷ 7	7	8	6	14
70 ÷ 7	7	63	10	49

The 9-times table				
1 × 9	0	9	10	90
6 × 9	51	52	53	54
9 × 9	72	81	93	99
7 × 9	62	63	72	73
45 ÷ 9	4	5	6	7
27 ÷ 9	2	3	4	5
90 ÷ 9	7	8	9	10

2. **Choose three answers from the 9-times table. Write them down.**

_____

Add the digits in each answer. _____

What do you notice about each total?

_____

Times-table quiz

You can use multiplication facts that you already know to work out others. For example, if you know that 3 × 4 = 12, you also know that 30 × 4 = 120.

Circle the correct answer for each of these questions.

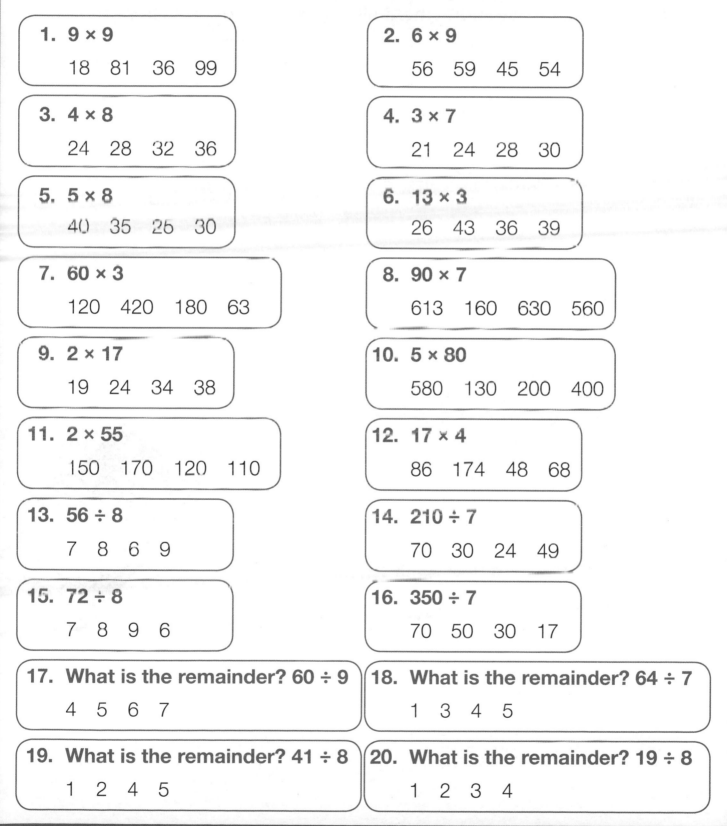

1. 9 × 9

   18   81   36   99

2. 6 × 9

   56   59   45   54

3. 4 × 8

   24   28   32   36

4. 3 × 7

   21   24   28   30

5. 5 × 8

   40   35   26   30

6. 13 × 3

   26   43   36   39

7. 60 × 3

   120   420   180   63

8. 90 × 7

   613   160   630   560

9. 2 × 17

   19   24   34   38

10. 5 × 80

   580   130   200   400

11. 2 × 55

   150   170   120   110

12. 17 × 4

   86   174   48   68

13. 56 ÷ 8

   7   8   6   9

14. 210 ÷ 7

   70   30   24   49

15. 72 ÷ 8

   7   8   9   6

16. 350 ÷ 7

   70   50   30   17

17. What is the remainder? 60 ÷ 9

   4   5   6   7

18. What is the remainder? 64 ÷ 7

   1   3   4   5

19. What is the remainder? 41 ÷ 8

   1   2   4   5

20. What is the remainder? 19 ÷ 8

   1   2   3   4

Times-table problems

You can use multiplication facts that you already know to work out others.
For example, to solve 50×3
$50 = 5 \times 10$. So $50 \times 3 = 5 \times 3 \times 10 = 15 \times 10 = 150$.

1. **Work out these questions mentally. Allow five seconds per question.**

    a. $6 \times 7 =$

    b. $5 \times 8 =$

    c. $9 \times 3 =$

    d. $40 \times 7 =$

    e. $50 \times 6 =$

    f. $2 \times 90 =$

2. **I save 80p per week. How much money will I have after 9 weeks?**

    _____

3. **Stickers cost 90p a packet. How much will 6 packets cost?** _____

4. **Chocolate bars are in packets of 6. How many packets do I need to buy for 40 children?** _____

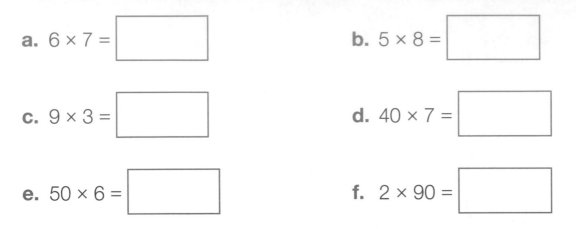

5. **My plant has grown 8cm each week.**

    It is now 32cm tall. How old is it? _____

6. **Answer these questions.**

    a. $56 \div 7 =$

    b. $64 \div 8 =$

Mental recall up to 12 × 12

Say the 11-times table. Write it down. Can you see a pattern in the answers? How can this help you remember it? Repeat for the 12-times table.

Match the calculation to its correct answer in each set.

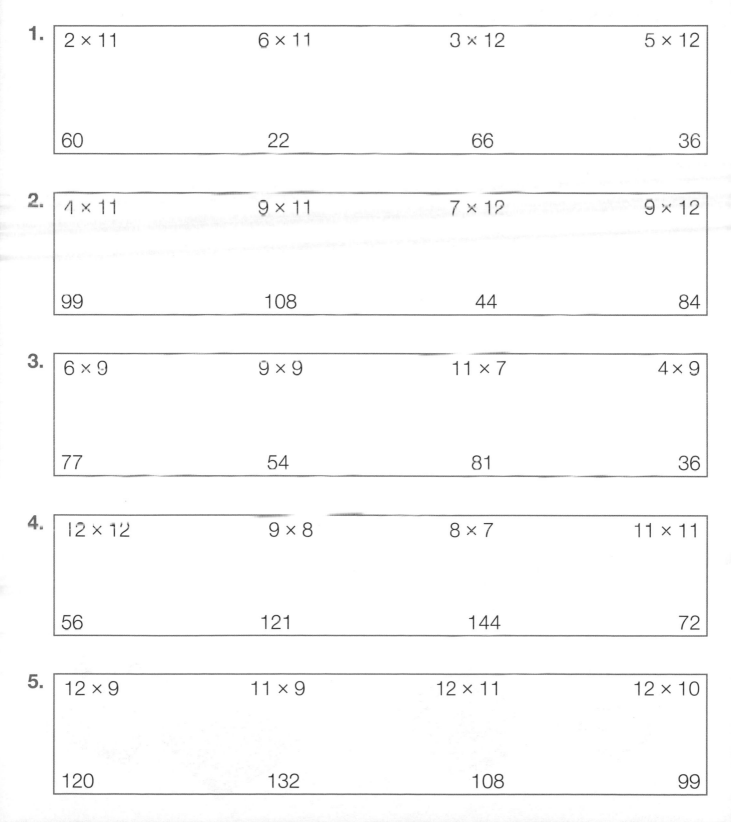

1.

2 × 11	6 × 11	3 × 12	5 × 12
60	22	66	36

2.

4 × 11	9 × 11	7 × 12	9 × 12
99	108	44	84

3.

6 × 9	9 × 9	11 × 7	4 × 9
77	54	81	36

4.

12 × 12	9 × 8	8 × 7	11 × 11
56	121	144	72

5.

12 × 9	11 × 9	12 × 11	12 × 10
120	132	108	99

Doubling and halving

If you know that double 6 = 12, you can use it to work out double 60 = 120.
If you know that half of 16 = 8, you can also work out that half of 160 = 80.

Answer these questions. Write down the number sentences or jottings you use to work out the answers.

1. Double 70

_____

2. Half of 140

_____

3. Double 16

_____

4. Half of 32

_____

5. Double 56

_____

6. Half of 112

_____

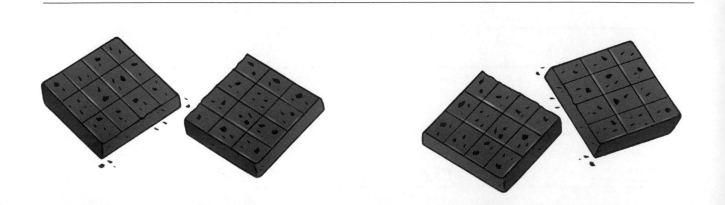

Know one fact, know them all

You can use doubling and halving to find facts you don't know.
If you know $5 \times 2 = 10$, you can double it to find $10 \times 2 = 20$.
If you know $80 \div 4 = 20$, then you can work out $40 \div 4 = 10$.

Use doubling and halving to complete these number sentences.

1. a. $4 \times 2 = 8$

$$\boxed{} \times 2 = 16$$

b. $16 \div 2 = 8$

$$\boxed{} \div 2 = 4$$

2. a. $4 \times 10 = 40$

$$\boxed{} \times 10 = 80$$

b. $80 \div 10 = 8$

$$\boxed{} \div 10 = 4$$

3. a. $5 \times 6 = 30$

$$\boxed{} \times 3 - 15$$

b. $15 \div 3 = 5$

$$\boxed{} \div 6 = 5$$

4. Write similar examples of your own.

_____

_____

Use what you know!

A multiple is a number that can be divided by another number, without a remainder. It is the product of two factors.

For example, 9 is a multiple of 3.

The 4th multiple of 6 is the same as 4 × 6 = 24.

Circle the correct answer each time.

1. **What is the third multiple of 8?**

    16   20   (24)   30

2. **What is the sixth multiple of 2?**

    2   5   (12)   20

3. **What is the ninth multiple of 7?**

    54   (63)   67   79

4. **Tick the calculation that you would do to find the 5th multiple of 25?**

    Add the 5th multiple of 10 to the 5th multiple of 5.   ☒

    Add the 5th multiple of 20 to the 5th multiple of 5.   ☑

    Add the 5th multiple of 15 to the 5th multiple of 5.   ☒

5. **What is 560 divided by 7?**

    (80)   90   10   70

6. **What is 210 divided by 3?**

    90   80   (70)   18

7. **What is 810 divided by 9?**

    100   (90)   110   80

Factors

A factor is a number which, when multiplied with another number, produces a whole number.

For example, 5 and 6 are factors of 30. So are 3 and 10.
5 × 6 = 30 and 3 × 10 = 30.

Any number that **goes exactly** into 30 will be a factor of 30.

Look at the numbers in the middle of each big X. Circle the factors of the number in the middle of each big X.

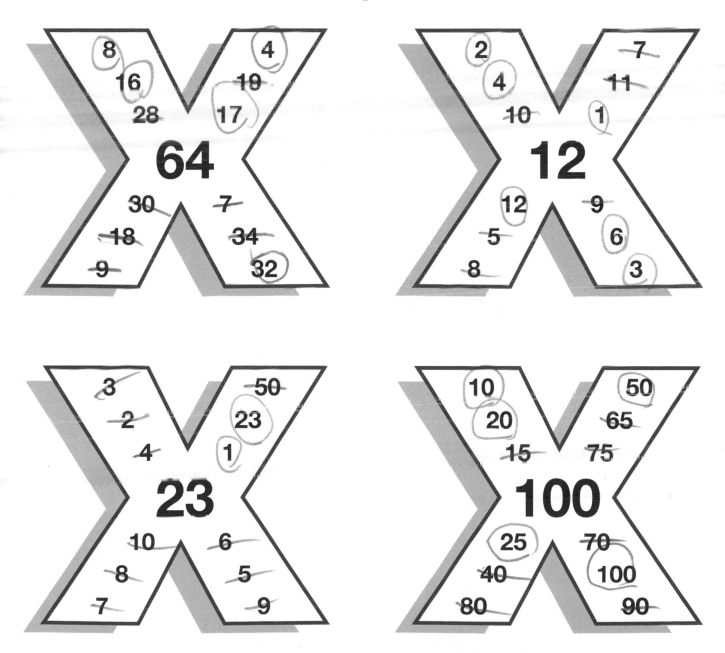

Partitioning when multiplying (1)

Partitioning teen numbers into 10s and 1s can make it easier to multiply.
For example, to solve 16×7.

16 can be partitioned into **10 + 6**.

We know **10 × 7** = 70 and **6 × 7** = 42. 70 + 42 = 112, so $16 \times 7 = 112$.

Use multiplication and division facts to work out these calculations. Show your working.

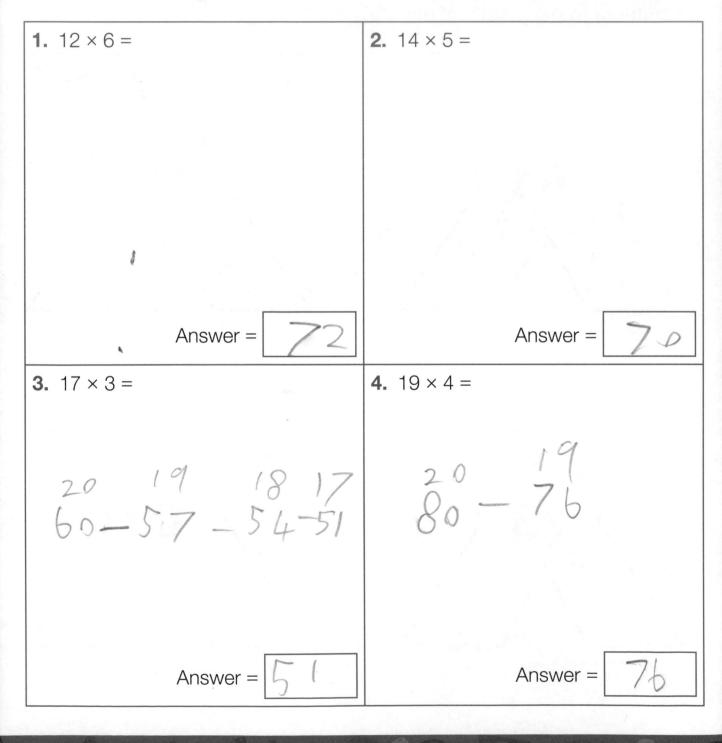

1. $12 \times 6 =$

Answer = 72

2. $14 \times 5 =$

Answer = 70

3. $17 \times 3 =$

20   19   18   17
60 — 57 — 54 — 51

Answer = 51

4. $19 \times 4 =$

20   19
80 — 76

Answer = 76

Partitioning when multiplying (2)

Partitioning numbers into 10s and 1s can make it easier to multiply 2-digit by 1-digit numbers. For example, to solve 42 × 8.

42 can be partitioned into **40 + 2**.

40 × 8 = 320 and **2** × 8 = 16. 320 + 16 = 336 so 42 × 8 = 336.

Use partitioning to work out these calculations. Show your working.

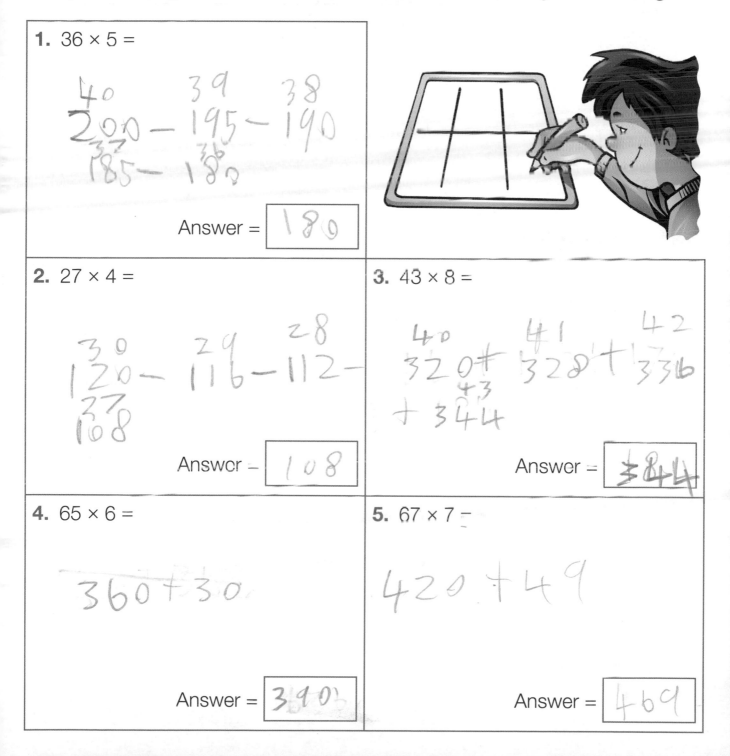

1. 36 × 5 =

40   39   38
200 — 195 — 190
  37   36
185 — 180

Answer = 180

2. 27 × 4 =

30   29   28
120 — 116 — 112 —
  27
108

Answer = 108

3. 43 × 8 =

40   41   42
320 + 328 + 336
      43
+ 344

Answer = 384

4. 65 × 6 =

360 + 30

Answer = 390

5. 67 × 7 =

420 + 49

Answer = 469

Partitioning when multiplying (3)

This example shows a way of thinking that may help you when partitoning and multiplying 2-digit numbers. $46 \times 3 = 40 \times 3 + 6 \times 3 = 120 + 18 = 138$.

1. **Write out your thinking stages as you do these problems. Use the example above to help you.**

   a. 43×2 _____

   b. 3×23 _____

   c. 32×4 _____

   d. 2×44 _____

   e. 27×2 _____

2. **Try and think in the same way as you work out the answers to the following calculations.**

   a. $56 \times 2 =$ ⬚   **b.** $4 \times 41 =$ ⬚   **c.** $18 \times 6 =$ ⬚

   d. $5 \times 23 =$ ⬚   **e.** $26 \times 8 =$ ⬚   **f.** $3 \times 32 =$ ⬚

   g. $34 \times 5 =$ ⬚   **h.** $8 \times 14 =$ ⬚   **i.** $35 \times 4 =$ ⬚

   j. $2 \times 74 =$ ⬚   **k.** $47 \times 3 =$ ⬚   **l.** $4 \times 48 =$ ⬚

3. **Read these questions and work out the correct answers.**

   a. If a box has a mass of 18kg, what is the total mass of five boxes?

   _____

   b. A newspaper costs 35p. What would the price of six papers be?

   _____

4. **Work out the answers to the calculations below. Draw lines to join the multiplications that give the same answer.**

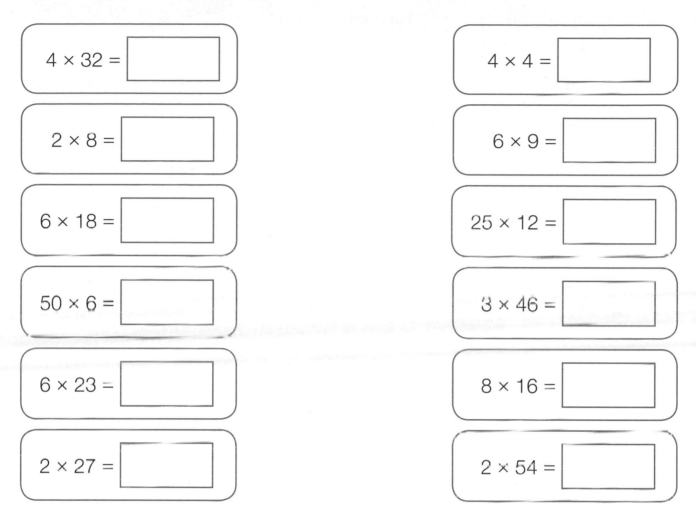

4 × 32 = [ ]

2 × 8 = [ ]

6 × 18 = [ ]

50 × 6 = [ ]

6 × 23 = [ ]

2 × 27 = [ ]

4 × 4 = [ ]

6 × 9 = [ ]

25 × 12 = [ ]

3 × 46 = [ ]

8 × 16 = [ ]

2 × 54 = [ ]

5. **Make up two pairs for yourself.**

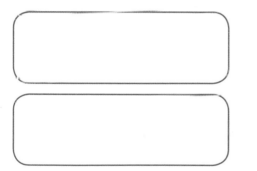

6. **Now look at this: 15 × 8 = 30 × 4 = 60 × 2 = 120 × 1**
   Can you explore the following products in the same way, so that they end with something multiplied by 1?

   a. 14 × 8 = _____

   b. 17 × 6 = _____

Using related multiplication and division facts

Multiplication is the opposite (inverse) of division.

We know $4 \times 3 = 12$, so $12 \div 3 = 4$ and $12 \div 4 = 3$.

If you have worked out a multiplication fact, then you also know related division facts (using the same numbers).

1. **Look at the example below and then write out the other problems in the same way.**

$8 \times 7 =$ **56, $7 \times 8 = 56$, $56 \div 8 = 7$, $56 \div 7 = 8$**

   a. $13 \times 3 =$ _____

   b. $4 \times 12 =$ _____

   c. $9 \times 7 =$ _____

   d. $6 \times 9 =$ _____

   e. $4 \times 8 =$ _____

Work out these sets of problems. The answers can already be seen if you look closely!

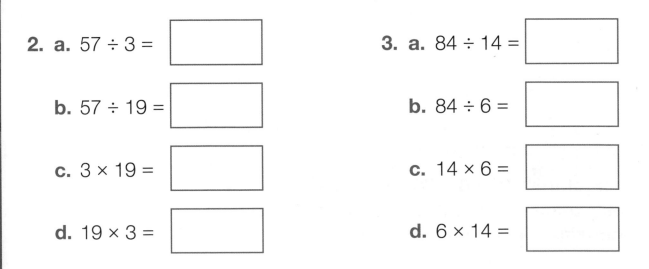

2. a. $57 \div 3 =$ ⬚   **3. a.** $84 \div 14 =$ ⬚

   b. $57 \div 19 =$ ⬚   **b.** $84 \div 6 =$ ⬚

   c. $3 \times 19 =$ ⬚   **c.** $14 \times 6 =$ ⬚

   d. $19 \times 3 =$ ⬚   **d.** $6 \times 14 =$ ⬚

How close can you get?

Use what you know to estimate answers.

You know there are ten 10s in 100. Use this to estimate how many 20s or 30s there are in 100. $100 \div 10 = 10$, so $100 \div 20 = 5$.

1. **What whole number does each of these numbers have to be multiplied by to get as close as possible to 100? Show your workings.**

18	34
29	**14**

Multiplying 3 small numbers mentally

You can multiply numbers in any order and the answer will be the same. This is called **commutativity**.

So 3 × 5 × 2 is the same as saying 5 × 2 × 3. The answer is still 30. Rearranging the numbers like this is called the **associative law**.

Use the associative law to help you rewrite and multiply these problems.

1. 6 × 7 × 4 = _____

2. 8 × 5 × 3 = _____

3. 9 × 2 × 6 = _____

4. 10 × 8 × 4 = _____

5. 3 × 6 × 7 = _____

6. 8 × 6 × 2 = _____

7. 4 × 3 × 2 = _____

8. 5 × 11 × 2 = _____

9. 7 × 12 × 3 = _____

Choosing the best order

Sometimes a multiplication looks difficult. For example, 2 × 17 × 5.
But if you multiply the numbers in a different order it becomes easier.
2 × 5 = 10, 10 × 17 = 170.

1. **Choose three numbers from the box below. Write them in the first column.**

$$2 \quad 3 \quad 4 \quad 6 \quad 7 \quad 8 \quad 9 \quad 10 \quad 11 \quad 12$$

2. **Now choose the easiest order to multiply them. The first one has been done for you.**

My numbers	My multiplication and answer
2, 4, 12	4 × 12 × 2: 4 × 12 = 48, 48 × 2 = 96

Multiplying and dividing by 10 or 100

When you multiply by 10, all the digits move one place to the left. 0 is used as a place holder.

100s	10s	1s		100s	10s	1s
	2	6	×10	2	6	0

When you divide by 10, all the digits move one place to the right.

100s	10s	1s		100s	10s	1s
2	6	0	÷10		2	6

When you multiply or divide by 100 all the digits move two places to the left or right. 0 is used as a place holder. So 26 × 100 = 2600 and 2600 ÷ 100 = 26.

1. **Answer these problems.**

    a. 34 × 10 = _____

    b. 29 × 100 = _____

    c. 6800 ÷ 10 = _____

    d. 3100 ÷ 100 = _____

2. **What number is 100 times bigger than 42?**

    _____

3. **What number is 10 times smaller than 830?**

    _____

4. **What operation do I need to change 5600 to 56?**

    _____

5. **Change 845p to pounds and pence.**

    _____

6. Circle the number on the right that is 10 times bigger than the number on the left.

×10

9	99	90	999	19	909
32	332	320	3200	230	323
56	556	5600	565	5650	560
122	1220	1210	1200	2100	1222
376	3670	3376	3760	3067	3700

7. Circle the number on the right that is 100 times bigger than the number on the left.

×100

4	44	400	404	444	4000
19	190	119	1990	1900	1009
56	5560	560	5600	5655	56000
37	3770	3007	3737	3700	3307
89	889	9880	8980	890	8900

8. Circle the number on the right that is 10 times smaller than the number on the left.

÷10

50	15	55	500	5	25
220	22	200	202	20	2
640	6400	64	6	46	60
2300	230	223	320	23	203
4120	410	420	400	41	412

Multiplying by 1 and 0

If you multiply a number by 1, the answer will be the same number as the number you are multiplying. For example, 4 × 1 = 4 (since 1 lot of 4 = 4).

If you multiply a number by 0, the answer is always 0. For example, 4 × 0 = 0 (since 0 lots of 4 = 0).

1. **Write the answers to these multiplications.**

   a. 6 × 1 =

   b. 45 × 1 =

   c. 6 × 4 × 1 =

   d. 1 × 7 × 5 =

   e. 450 × 1 =

   f. 1 × 18 =

   g. 72 × 1 =

   h. 2 × 3 × 1 =

   i. 1 × 12 × 6 =

   j. 872 × 1 =

2. **Now try these.**

   a. 1 × 0 =

   b. 86 × 0 =

   c. 7 × 3 × 0 =

   d. 15 × 0 =

   e. 0 × 240 =

   f. 11 × 5 × 0 =

3. **Hannah bought 1 bag of 50g sweets.**

   What was their total mass?

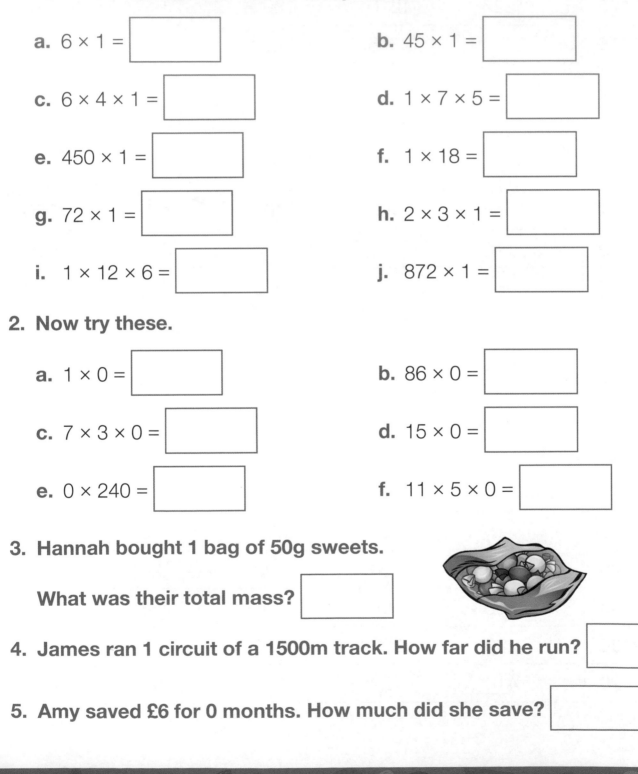

4. **James ran 1 circuit of a 1500m track. How far did he run?**

5. **Amy saved £6 for 0 months. How much did she save?**

Dividing by 1

If you divide a number by 1, the answer will always be the same number as the number you are dividing. For example, $6 \div 1 = 6$ (since there are 6 groups of 1 in 6).

1. **Choose a number from the box. Write it in the table. Divide it by 1 and write the division calculation. Then write your answer. Do this five times.**

$$6 \quad 12 \quad 25 \quad 49 \quad 180 \quad 3542$$

My number	My division	My answer

2. **Fill in the missing numbers.**

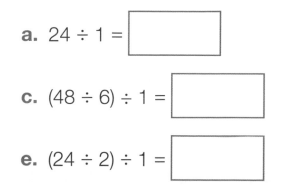

a. $24 \div 1 = \boxed{}$

c. $(48 \div 6) \div 1 = \boxed{}$

e. $(24 \div 2) \div 1 = \boxed{}$

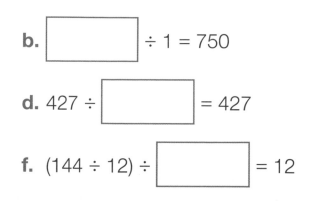

b. $\boxed{} \div 1 = 750$

d. $427 \div \boxed{} = 427$

f. $(144 \div 12) \div \boxed{} = 12$

Short multiplication

This is the written method for short multiplication:

$$
\begin{array}{r}
8\,3 \\
\times \quad 9 \\
\hline
7\,4\,7 \\
{\scriptstyle 2}
\end{array}
$$

Multiply the 1s: $3 \times 9 = 27$. Write 7 in the 1s column and write the 2 (10s) under the 10s column.

Multiply the 10s: $8 \times 9 = 72$, then add on the additional 2 underneath = 74. Write 4 in the 10s column and 7 in the 100s column.

1. **Use a written method of short multiplication to solve these problems.**

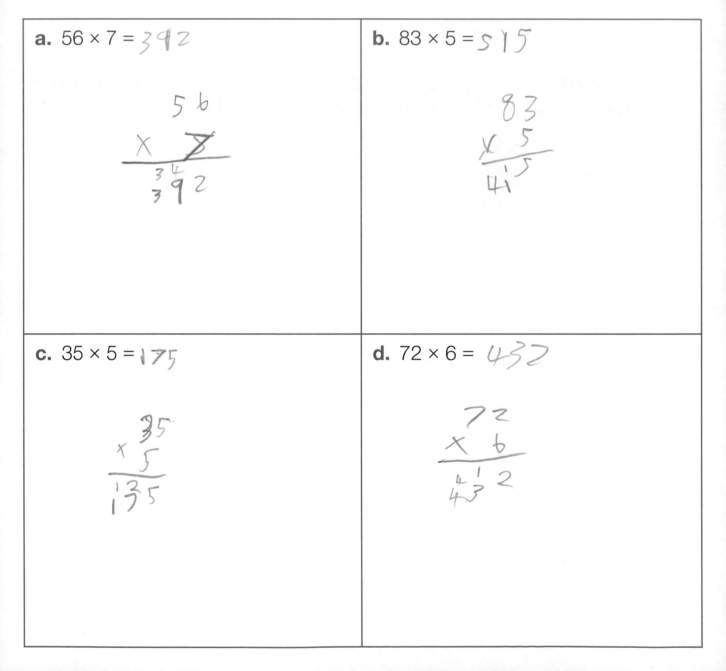

a. $56 \times 7 = 392$

$$
\begin{array}{r}
5\,6 \\
\times \quad 7 \\
\hline
3\,{\scriptstyle 4}\,9\,2 \\
{\scriptstyle 3}
\end{array}
$$

b. $83 \times 5 = 515$

$$
\begin{array}{r}
8\,3 \\
\times \quad 5 \\
\hline
4\,{\scriptstyle 1}\,5
\end{array}
$$

c. $35 \times 5 = 175$

$$
\begin{array}{r}
3\,5 \\
\times \quad 5 \\
\hline
1\,3\,5
\end{array}
$$

d. $72 \times 6 = 432$

$$
\begin{array}{r}
7\,2 \\
\times \quad 6 \\
\hline
4\,{\scriptstyle 1}\,3\,2
\end{array}
$$

2. Choose a number from each box. Multiply your numbers together using a written method of short multiplication.
Do this three more times.

| 34   76   79   58 | | 6   5   4   3 |

Short multiplication with larger numbers

Here is another example of the written method for multiplication.

Multiply the 1s: $6 \times 7 = 42$. Write 2 in the 1s column and write the 4 (10s) under the 10s column.

$$
\begin{array}{r}
2\,3\,6 \\
\times \quad 7 \\
\hline
1\,6\,5\,2 \\
{\scriptstyle 2\ 4}
\end{array}
$$

Multiply the 10s: $3 \times 7 = 21$, then add on the additional 4 underneath = 25. Write 5 in the 10s column and write the 2 (100s) under the 100s column.

Multiply the 100s: $2 \times 7 = 14$, then add on the additional 2 underneath = 16. Write 6 in the 100s column and 1 in the 1000s column.

1. Use a written method to solve the following problems.

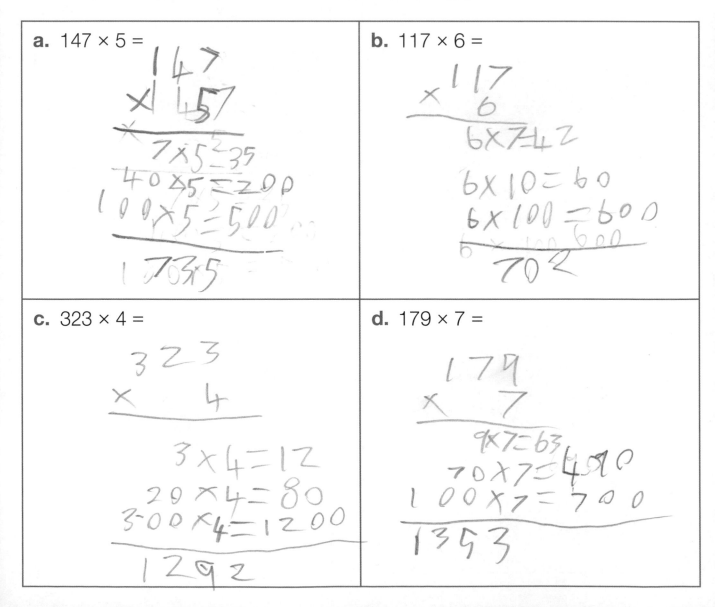

a. $147 \times 5 =$

147
$\times \ 57$

$7 \times 5 = 35$
$40 \times 5 = 200$
$100 \times 5 = 500$

1703×5

b. $117 \times 6 =$

$\times \ 117$
6

$6 \times 7 = 42$
$6 \times 10 = 60$
$6 \times 100 = 600$
$6 \times 100 \ 600$

702

c. $323 \times 4 =$

323
$\times \quad 4$

$3 \times 4 = 12$
$20 \times 4 = 80$
$300 \times 4 = 1200$

1292

d. $179 \times 7 =$

179
$\times \quad 7$

$9 \times 7 = 63$
$70 \times 7 = 490$
$100 \times 7 = 700$

1353

 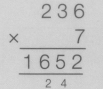

Short division

This is the written method for short division:

$$6 \overline{)9\ {}^{3}6}\quad \begin{array}{c}1\ 6\end{array}$$

Start by dividing the 10s: $9 \div 6 = 1$, with 3 remainder. Put a small 3 before the six 1s, making thirty-six 1s.

Next divide the 1s: $36 \div 6 = 6$. The answer is 16.

1. **Use a written method of short division to solve these problems.**

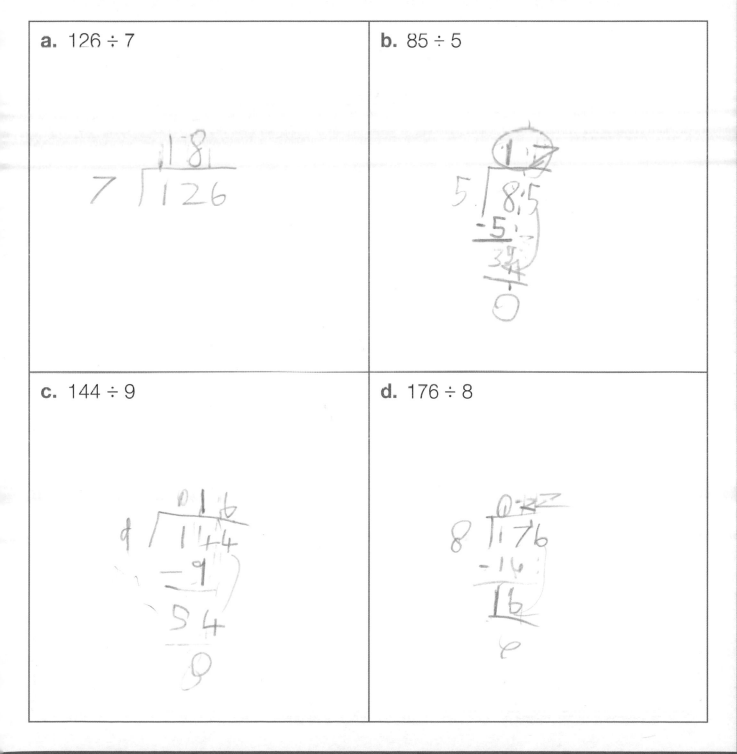

a. $126 \div 7$

b. $85 \div 5$

c. $144 \div 9$

d. $176 \div 8$

Focus on fractions

Fractions are used all around us.

Think about how you tell the time (**half** past four, **quarter** to five). Look at recipe books ($\frac{1}{2}$ teaspoon). We use fractions in other ways, too (**half** the class are girls and **half** are boys).

1. **Look around your home to see how many examples of fractions you can find. Look in the food cupboard or in a newspaper, and ask an adult for some ideas.**

    Write, draw or cut out and stick your examples here. Remember to ask permission before cutting up any newspapers or packets!

Fraction shapes

Count the number of parts in the larger shape (denominator).

Count the number of parts in the smaller shape (numerator).

If there are 5 parts in the larger shape and 2 parts in the smaller shape, the fraction is $\frac{2}{5}$.

1. **Write what fraction the smaller shape is of the larger shape.**

Fractions of quantities

What is $\frac{1}{8}$ of 32? 32 ÷ 8 = 4.
What is $\frac{3}{8}$ of 32? Multiply the total for $\frac{1}{8}$ (32 ÷ 8 = 4) by 3.
So $\frac{3}{8}$ of 32 = 4 × 3 = 12

Read each question and circle the correct answer.

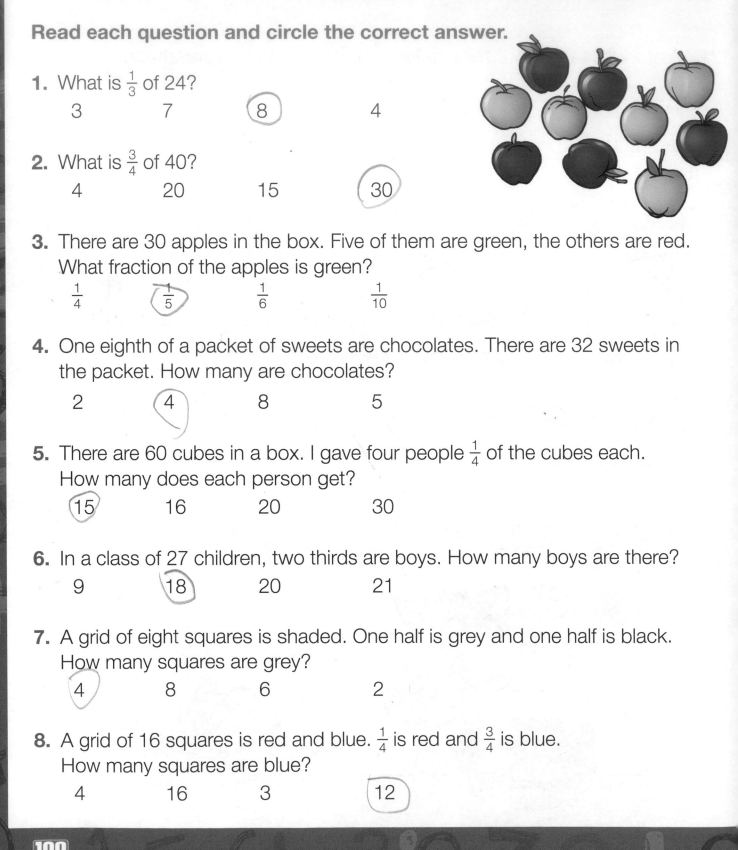

1. What is $\frac{1}{3}$ of 24?

   3   7   (8)   4

2. What is $\frac{3}{4}$ of 40?

   4   20   15   (30)

3. There are 30 apples in the box. Five of them are green, the others are red.
   What fraction of the apples is green?

   $\frac{1}{4}$ ($\frac{1}{5}$) $\frac{1}{6}$ $\frac{1}{10}$

4. One eighth of a packet of sweets are chocolates. There are 32 sweets in
   the packet. How many are chocolates?

   2   (4)   8   5

5. There are 60 cubes in a box. I gave four people $\frac{1}{4}$ of the cubes each.
   How many does each person get?

   (15)   16   20   30

6. In a class of 27 children, two thirds are boys. How many boys are there?

   9   (18)   20   21

7. A grid of eight squares is shaded. One half is grey and one half is black.
   How many squares are grey?

   (4)   8   6   2

8. A grid of 16 squares is red and blue. $\frac{1}{4}$ is red and $\frac{3}{4}$ is blue.
   How many squares are blue?

   4   16   3   (12)

Less than or more than $\frac{1}{2}$?

HTO.thth
000.7.
010.1

A fraction is $\frac{1}{2}$ when the numerator is half the denominator such as $\frac{3}{6}$, $\frac{5}{10}$.
So if the numerator is less than half the denominator, it is less than $\frac{1}{2}$, as with $\frac{5}{12}$ or $\frac{7}{16}$.

A decimal is more than $\frac{1}{2}$ if there is more than 0.5. So 0.51 is more than $\frac{1}{2}$, as is 0.7.

1. **You will need some coloured pencils or pens. Colour these fractions according to the instructions below.**
   - Less than $\frac{1}{2}$ colour in red.
   - More than $\frac{1}{2}$ colour in yellow.

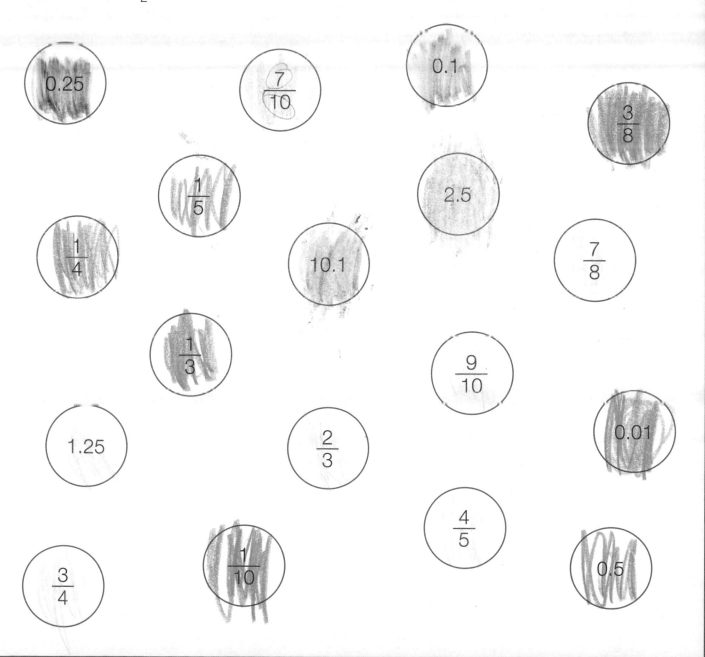

Match equivalent fractions

Equivalent fractions are fractions that have the same value.

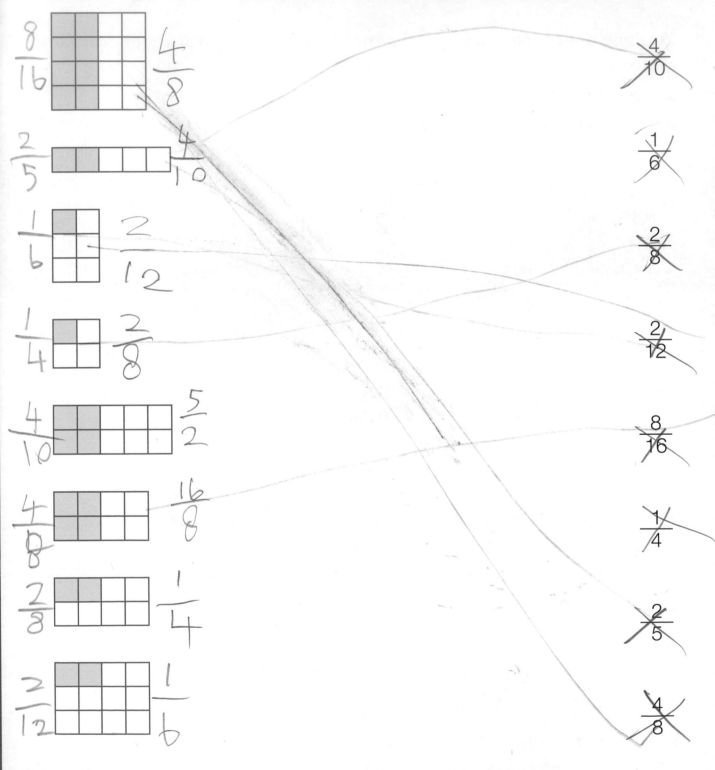

is equivalent to

1. Draw lines to join the shapes with matching equivalent fractions.

$\frac{8}{16}$ $\frac{4}{8}$ $\frac{4}{10}$

$\frac{2}{5}$ $\frac{4}{10}$ $\frac{1}{6}$

$\frac{1}{6}$ $\frac{2}{12}$ $\frac{2}{8}$

$\frac{1}{4}$ $\frac{2}{8}$ $\frac{2}{12}$

$\frac{4}{10}$ $\frac{5}{2}$ $\frac{8}{16}$

$\frac{4}{8}$ $\frac{16}{8}$ $\frac{1}{4}$

$\frac{2}{8}$ $\frac{1}{4}$ $\frac{2}{5}$

$\frac{2}{12}$ $\frac{1}{6}$ $\frac{4}{8}$

Fraction equivalents

To find an equivalent fraction of another fraction, multiply the top and bottom numbers by the same number. For example, to solve $\frac{1}{3} = \frac{?}{15}$

You multiply 3 (the denominator) by 5 to get 15. So multiply the numerator by 5 too: $1 \times 5 = 5$

So $\frac{1}{3}$ is equivalent to $\frac{5}{15}$.

1. **What two equivalent fractions can you use to describe how much of each of these squares is shaded?**

   $\frac{6}{8}$ $\frac{3}{4}$

2. **Complete these fractions.**

   a. $\dfrac{8}{16} = \dfrac{1}{2}$

   b. $\dfrac{2}{16} = \dfrac{1}{8}$

   c. $\dfrac{4}{16} = \dfrac{1}{4}$

   d. $\dfrac{2}{8} = \dfrac{1}{4}$

   e. $\dfrac{12}{16} = \dfrac{3}{4}$

   f. $\dfrac{3}{8} = \dfrac{6}{16}$

3. **Write some fractions that are equivalent to $\frac{1}{3}$.**

   $\dfrac{2}{6}$ $\dfrac{3}{9}$ $\dfrac{100}{300}$ $\dfrac{4}{12}$ $\dfrac{1000}{3000}$

4. **How can you check whether two fractions are equivalent?**

   $\frac{1}{3} = \frac{1}{2}$? You have to have same denominator $\frac{3}{6}$ & $\frac{3}{4}$

5. **Place these numbers on the number line.**

   2 $\frac{1}{2}$ 1 0 1½ 2.5 $\frac{1}{4}$ $\frac{3}{4}$ 1.25 1.75 2.25 2.75 3

   0 $\frac{1}{4}$ $\frac{1}{2}$ $\frac{3}{4}$ 1 1.25 1.5 1.75 2 2.25 2.5 2.75 3

Adding fractions to make 1

A fraction = 1 if the denominator and numerator are the same: $\frac{7}{7} = \frac{2}{2} = \frac{30}{30} = 1$.
$\frac{1}{4} + \frac{3}{4} = 1$ (add the numerators: 3 + 1 = 4).

1. **Each of these fractions has a pair that totals 1. Match them together by drawing a line. The first one has been done for you.**

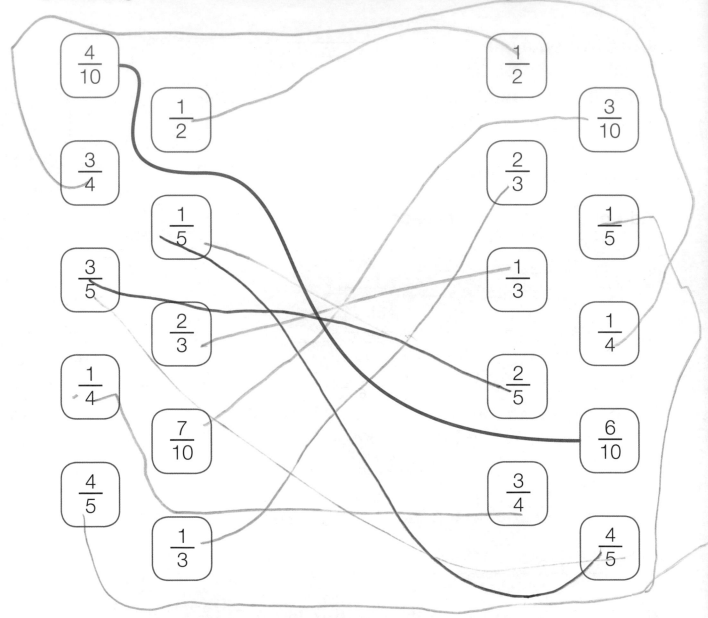

2. **Which fraction would you need to add to each of these to make 1?**

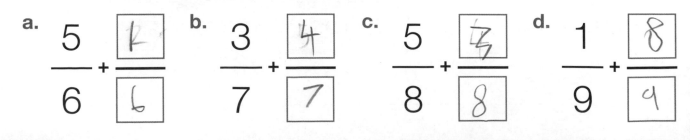

a. $\dfrac{5}{6} + \dfrac{1}{6}$ b. $\dfrac{3}{7} + \dfrac{4}{7}$ c. $\dfrac{5}{8} + \dfrac{3}{8}$ d. $\dfrac{1}{9} + \dfrac{8}{9}$

Adding and subtracting fractions

To add fractions, add the numerators. The denominator stays the same:
$\frac{4}{7} + \frac{2}{7} = \frac{6}{7}$

To subtract fractions, subtract the numerators. The denominator stays the same: $\frac{4}{7} - \frac{2}{7} = \frac{2}{7}$

1. Calculate the following.

a. 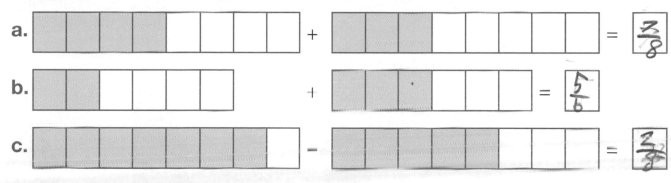 $= \boxed{\frac{3}{8}}$

b. $+$ $= \boxed{\frac{5}{6}}$

c. $-$ $= \boxed{\frac{2}{8}}$

2. Add or subtract to find each answer.

a. $\frac{1}{3} + \frac{2}{3} = \boxed{1}$

b. $\frac{2}{7} + \frac{4}{7} = \boxed{\frac{6}{7}}$

c. $\frac{9}{10} - \frac{4}{10} = \boxed{\frac{5}{10}}$

d. $\frac{5}{9} - \frac{2}{9} = \boxed{\frac{3}{9}}$

e. $\frac{3}{5} + \frac{1}{5} = \boxed{\frac{4}{5}}$

f. $\frac{2}{10} + \frac{6}{10} = \boxed{\frac{8}{10}}$

g. $\frac{3}{12} - \frac{1}{12} = \boxed{\frac{2}{12}}$

h. $\frac{6}{6} - \frac{6}{6} = \boxed{0}$

3. Calculate and then simplify each answer.

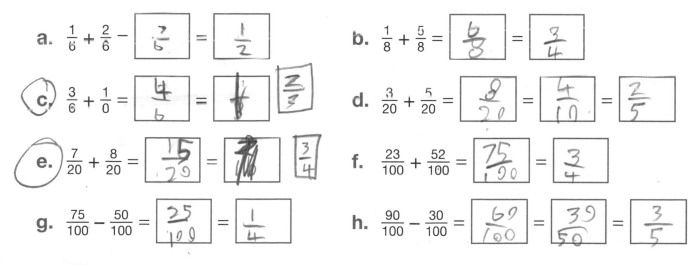

a. $\frac{1}{6} + \frac{2}{6} - \boxed{\frac{3}{6}} = \boxed{\frac{1}{2}}$

b. $\frac{1}{8} + \frac{5}{8} = \boxed{\frac{6}{8}} = \boxed{\frac{3}{4}}$

c. $\frac{3}{6} + \frac{1}{6} = \boxed{\frac{4}{6}} = \boxed{\frac{2}{3}}$

d. $\frac{3}{20} + \frac{5}{20} = \boxed{\frac{8}{20}} = \boxed{\frac{4}{10}} = \boxed{\frac{2}{5}}$

e. $\frac{7}{20} + \frac{8}{20} = \boxed{\frac{15}{20}} = \boxed{\frac{3}{4}}$

f. $\frac{23}{100} + \frac{52}{100} = \boxed{\frac{75}{100}} = \boxed{\frac{3}{4}}$

g. $\frac{75}{100} - \frac{50}{100} = \boxed{\frac{25}{100}} = \boxed{\frac{1}{4}}$

h. $\frac{90}{100} - \frac{30}{100} = \boxed{\frac{60}{100}} = \boxed{\frac{39}{50}} = \boxed{\frac{3}{5}}$

Fractions (including decimals)

Fraction and decimal equivalents (1)

These are the most common fraction and decimal equivalents. All fractions can be written as decimals.

Here are all the tenths, up to 1, as fractions and decimals.

$\frac{1}{4}$	$\frac{1}{2}$	$\frac{3}{4}$	1
0.25	0.5	0.75	1.0

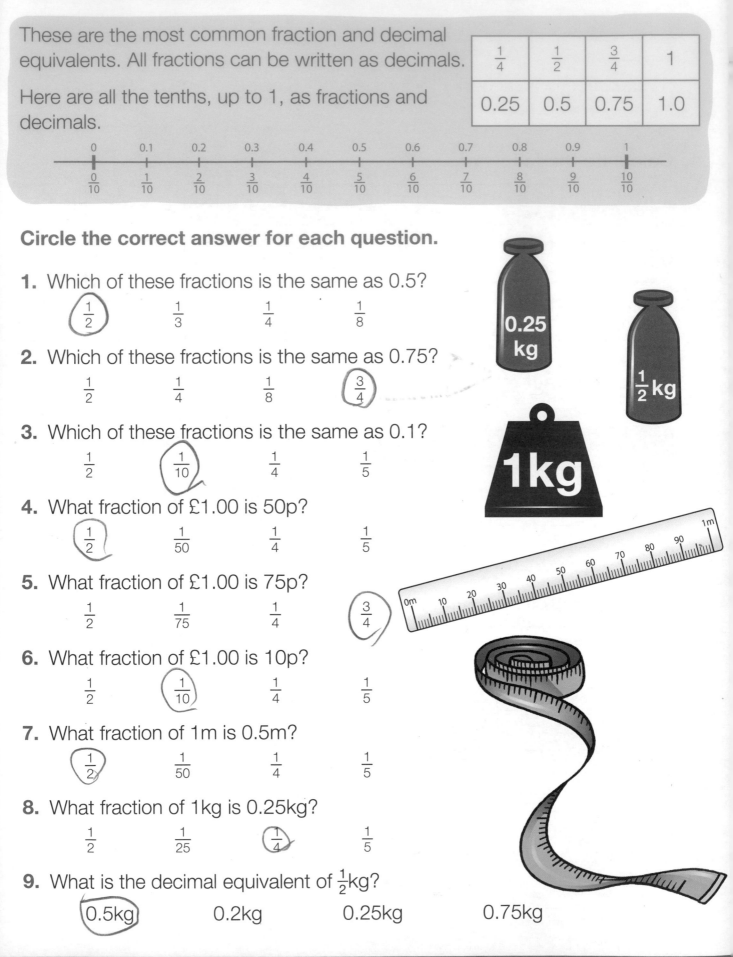

Circle the correct answer for each question.

1. Which of these fractions is the same as 0.5?

    (⃝$\frac{1}{2}$) $\frac{1}{3}$ $\frac{1}{4}$ $\frac{1}{8}$

2. Which of these fractions is the same as 0.75?

    $\frac{1}{2}$ $\frac{1}{4}$ $\frac{1}{8}$ (⃝$\frac{3}{4}$)

3. Which of these fractions is the same as 0.1?

    $\frac{1}{2}$ (⃝$\frac{1}{10}$) $\frac{1}{4}$ $\frac{1}{5}$

4. What fraction of £1.00 is 50p?

    (⃝$\frac{1}{2}$) $\frac{1}{50}$ $\frac{1}{4}$ $\frac{1}{5}$

5. What fraction of £1.00 is 75p?

    $\frac{1}{2}$ $\frac{1}{75}$ $\frac{1}{4}$ (⃝$\frac{3}{4}$)

6. What fraction of £1.00 is 10p?

    $\frac{1}{2}$ (⃝$\frac{1}{10}$) $\frac{1}{4}$ $\frac{1}{5}$

7. What fraction of 1m is 0.5m?

    (⃝$\frac{1}{2}$) $\frac{1}{50}$ $\frac{1}{4}$ $\frac{1}{5}$

8. What fraction of 1kg is 0.25kg?

    $\frac{1}{2}$ $\frac{1}{25}$ (⃝$\frac{1}{4}$) $\frac{1}{5}$

9. What is the decimal equivalent of $\frac{1}{2}$kg?

    (⃝0.5kg)   0.2kg   0.25kg   0.75kg

Fraction and decimal equivalents (2)

When matching decimals and fractions that also include whole numbers, the whole number stays the same, so you only need to look at the fractional part. For example, $1\frac{1}{2} = 1.5$ and $6\frac{3}{4} = 6.75$.

Match the calculation to its equivalent in each set.

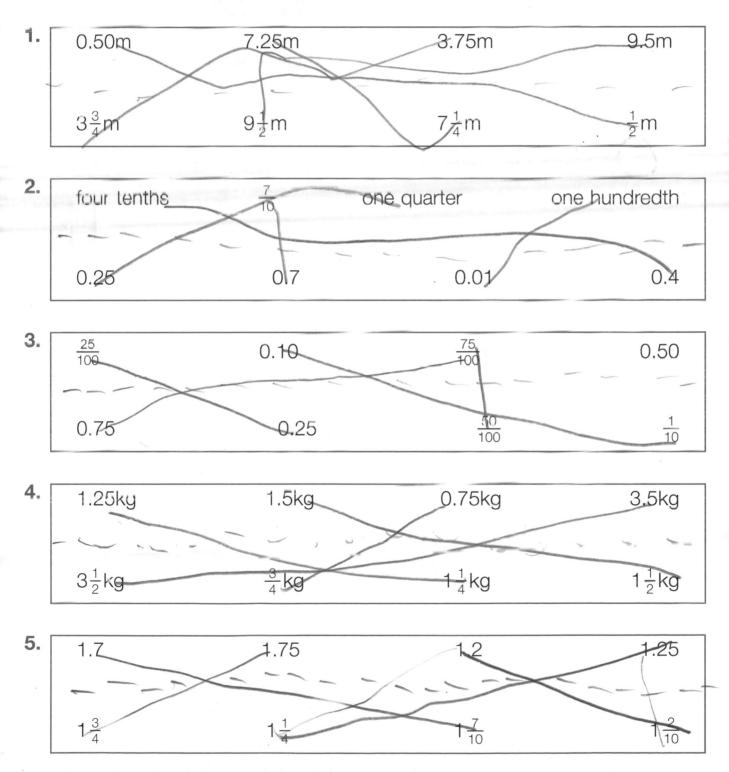

1. 0.50m   7.25m   3.75m   9.5m

   $3\frac{3}{4}$m $9\frac{1}{2}$m $7\frac{1}{4}$m $\frac{1}{2}$m

2. four tenths $\frac{7}{10}$ one quarter   one hundredth

   0.25   0.7   0.01   0.4

3. $\frac{25}{100}$ 0.10 $\frac{75}{100}$ 0.50

   0.75   0.25 $\frac{50}{100}$ $\frac{1}{10}$

4. 1.25kg   1.5kg   0.75kg   3.5kg

   $3\frac{1}{2}$kg $\frac{3}{4}$kg $1\frac{1}{4}$kg $1\frac{1}{2}$kg

5. 1.7   1.75   1.2   1.25

   $1\frac{3}{4}$ $1\frac{1}{4}$ $1\frac{7}{10}$ $1\frac{2}{10}$

Hundredths

One whole can be divided into 100 parts. Each part is called a **hundredth**.
One hundredth is written as $\frac{1}{100}$ or 0.01.
The position of a digit shows its value. For example, in 562.14 the 4 digit = $\frac{4}{100}$,
and 0.14 = $\frac{14}{100}$:

100s	10s	1s	.	0.1s	0.01s
5	6	2	.	1	4

1. **Fill in each small square in the 100-square until you have 100 hundredths.**

$\frac{1}{100}$	$\frac{2}{100}$	$\frac{3}{100}$	$\frac{4}{100}$	$\frac{5}{100}$	$\frac{6}{100}$	$\frac{7}{100}$	$\frac{8}{100}$	$\frac{9}{100}$	$\frac{10}{100}$
$\frac{11}{100}$	$\frac{12}{100}$	$\frac{13}{100}$	$\frac{14}{100}$	$\frac{15}{100}$					
				$\frac{35}{100}$					
						$\frac{47}{100}$			
							$\frac{58}{100}$		$\frac{60}{100}$
$\frac{61}{100}$				$\frac{65}{100}$					
								$\frac{79}{100}$	
	$\frac{82}{100}$								
		$\frac{93}{100}$				$\frac{97}{100}$			

Counting in hundredths

There are $\frac{100}{100}$ in 1 whole.

$\frac{10}{100} = \frac{1}{10} = 0.1$.

.H

$\frac{150}{100} = 1\frac{1}{2}$ or 1.5.

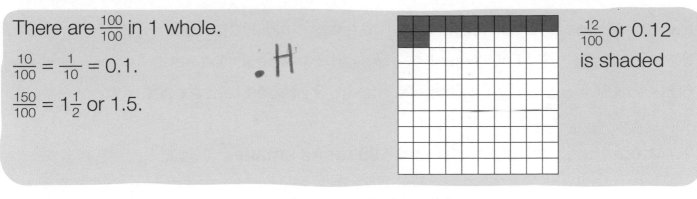

$\frac{12}{100}$ or 0.12 is shaded

1. **Use the hundredths square on page 86. Colour the fraction in, then write it as a decimal.**

   a. $\frac{3}{100}$ in red   0.03

   b. $\frac{10}{100}$ in blue   0.1

   c. $\frac{16}{100}$ in yellow   0.16

   d. $\frac{40}{100}$ in green   0.4

2. **Complete these fractions. Write the decimal equivalents in the last box.**

   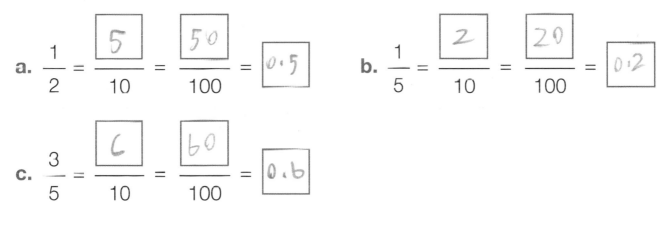

   a. $\dfrac{1}{2} = \dfrac{5}{10} = \dfrac{50}{100} = $ 0.5

   b. $\dfrac{1}{5} = \dfrac{2}{10} = \dfrac{20}{100} = $ 0.2

   c. $\dfrac{3}{5} = \dfrac{6}{10} = \dfrac{60}{100} = $ 0.6

3. **Write these as decimals.**

   a. $\frac{13}{100} = $ 0.13

   b. $\frac{43}{100} = $ 0.43

   c. $\frac{156}{100} = $ 1.56

4. **Write the decimal for each arrow.**

0.01   0.23   0.68   0.85

0   1

Dividing by 10 and 100

0.6 is 10 times smaller than 6 and 100 times smaller than 60.

60.0 ÷ **10** = 6   The digits have moved **1 place** to the right.

60.0 ÷ **100** = 0.6   The digits have moved **2 places** to the right.

1. **Make these amounts 10 and 100 times smaller.**

Amount	÷ 10	÷ 100
2780m	278m	2*78
6700km	670	617.
£43,000	4300	£430
4060g	406g	
9000p		90p

Amount	÷ 10	÷ 100
2430g		
3000p		
680g		
7500m		
£6000		

2. **Make these amounts 10 times smaller. You might need to add a decimal point.**

a. 8.7 _____

b. 92 _____

c. 36 _____

d. 410 _____

e. 89.7 _____

f. 28.3 _____

g. 8 _____

h. 1.4 _____

i. 701 _____

j. 6.9 _____

3. Join each number at the top to a number 100 times smaller, below. One has been done for you.

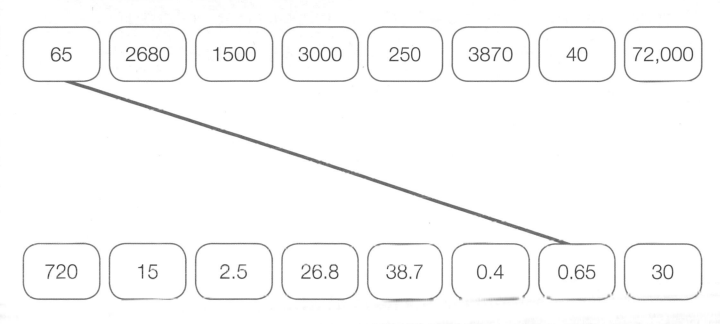

| 65 | 2680 | 1500 | 3000 | 250 | 3870 | 40 | 72,000 |

| 720 | 15 | 2.5 | 26.8 | 38.7 | 0.4 | 0.65 | 30 |

4. Complete these sentences.

a. 3.86 is _____ times smaller than 386.

b. 452 is _____ times smaller than 4520.

c. $\frac{1}{10}$ of 365 = _____

d. $\frac{1}{10}$ of 43 = _____

e. $\frac{1}{100}$ of 365 = _____

f. $\frac{1}{100}$ of 43 = _____

g. Class 4 raised £248 in a cake sale. A tenth of this money was spent on ingredients. How much was this? _____

h. Peter saved 864p. How much is that in pounds and pence? _____

i. Oscar walked 2651cm. How much is that is metres? _____

And in km? _____

Rounding decimals

To round a decimal to the nearest whole number, look at tenths digit.

If it is 5 or more, round up.   If it is less than 5, round down.

2.**36** rounded down = 2   2.**71** rounded up = 3.

1. Round these prices to the nearest pound.

a. £3.53 __4__   b. £9.99 __10__

c. £10.24 __10__   d. £0.65 __1__

2. Round these amounts to the nearest whole.

a. 3.6 hours __4__   b. 10.3 litres __10__

c. 5.8m __6__   d. 122.4 hours __122__

e. 25.5cm __26__   f. £1.75 __2__

g. 2.3 hours __2__   h. 7.7 litres __8__

3. Round each decimal to the nearest whole number.

40 [40] [40] [50] [50] 50

4. Round these heights to the nearest metre.

Landmark	Height	Nearest metre
Blackpool Tower	157.62m	158
Big Ben	95.73m	96
London Eye	135.26m	135
Humber Bridge	164.38m	164

Ordering decimal numbers

When ordering decimal numbers, start by ordering the whole numbers. For example, 4.2 is smaller than 5.2, because 4 is smaller than 5.

Then look at the tenths and order those. 0.1 is smaller than 0.6.

Finally look at the hundredths. 0.65 is bigger than 0.63.

Put the numbers or amounts in order of size, starting with the smallest.

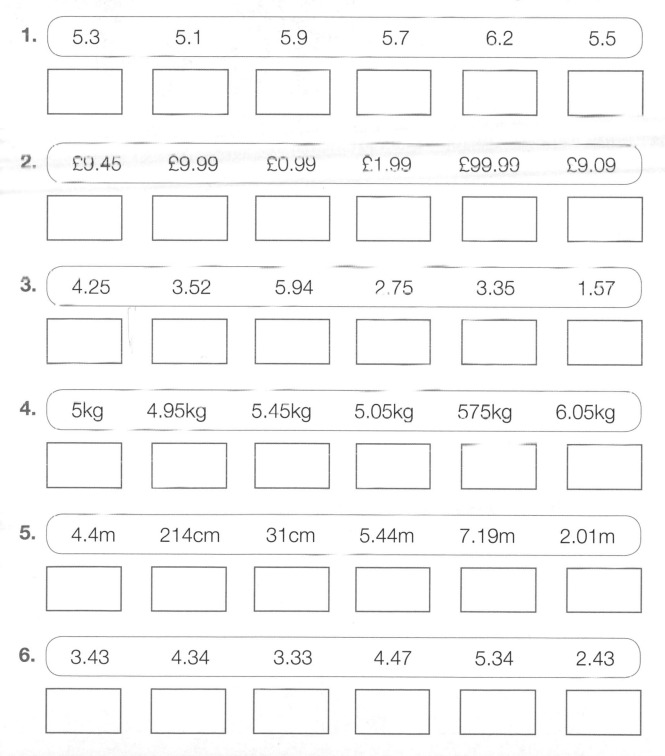

1. | 5.3 | 5.1 | 5.9 | 5.7 | 6.2 | 5.5 |

2. | £9.45 | £9.99 | £0.99 | £1.99 | £99.99 | £9.09 |

3. | 4.25 | 3.52 | 5.94 | 2.75 | 3.35 | 1.57 |

4. | 5kg | 4.95kg | 5.45kg | 5.05kg | 575kg | 6.05kg |

5. | 4.4m | 214cm | 31cm | 5.44m | 7.19m | 2.01m |

6. | 3.43 | 4.34 | 3.33 | 4.47 | 5.34 | 2.43 |

Converting lengths

You can record length using different units, such as millimetres (mm), centimetres (cm), metres (m) and kilometres (km).

1. **Complete this chart.**

	1 0	millimetres = 1 centimetre
	1 0 0	centimetres = 1 metre
	1 0 0 0	metres = 1 kilometre

2. **Write the lengths in the new units.**

a. 20mm = _2_ cm	**b.** 10cm = _0.1_ m
c. 3m = _300_ cm	**d.** 200m = _0.12_ km
e. 70cm = _700_ mm	**f.** 45cm = _4.5_ mm
g. 6km = _6000_ m	**h.** 8m = _800_ cm
i. 400mm = _40_ cm	**j.** 350cm = _3.5_ m

Comparing distances

When comparing lengths it is better to compare them using the same unit of length. You may have to convert some lengths to a different unit to do this.

Remember: 1000mm = 1m = 100cm.

1. **Find the shortest distance across the grid. You may move horizontally or vertically.**

Start

120cm	8m	2m	500cm	24m
120	*800*	*200*	*500*	*2400*
400cm	1.5m	17m	420cm	345cm
400	*150*	*1700*	*42000*	*345*
40mm	56cm	184cm	12.5m	320cm
40	*56*	*184*	*1250*	*320*

Finish

Find the perimeter

The perimeter is the total length around a shape. For a rectangle the perimeter is 2× length + 2× width.

For some shapes, you can split them into two or more rectangles to find the total perimeter.

For some shapes you will need to add the lengths of all the sides.

1. **Find the perimeter of each of these shapes.**

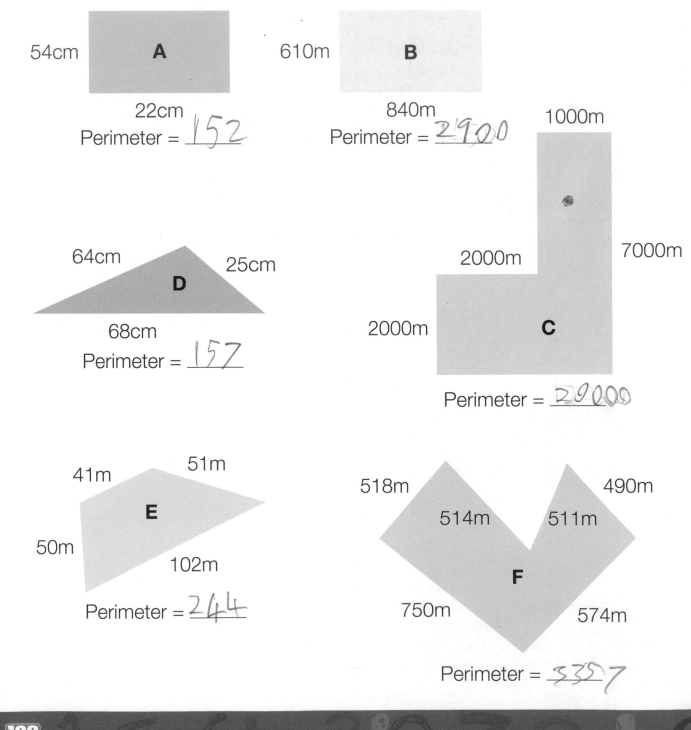

54cm **A**

22cm
Perimeter = _152_

610m **B**

840m
Perimeter = _2900_

1000m

2000m

7000m

2000m **C**

Perimeter = _29000_

64cm **D** 25cm

68cm
Perimeter = _157_

41m 51m

E

50m

102m
Perimeter = _244_

518m 514m 511m 490m

F

750m 574m

Perimeter = _3357_

Area and perimeter

The area of a rectangle = length × width.
The perimeter of a rectangle is 2× length + 2× width.

Class 4W's classroom needs a new carpet.
Use the plan shown below to answer the questions.
These are two-step problems. Think about what you need to work out first and then how to answer the question.

1. How much gripper rod do they need for the edge of the carpet?

aka fence

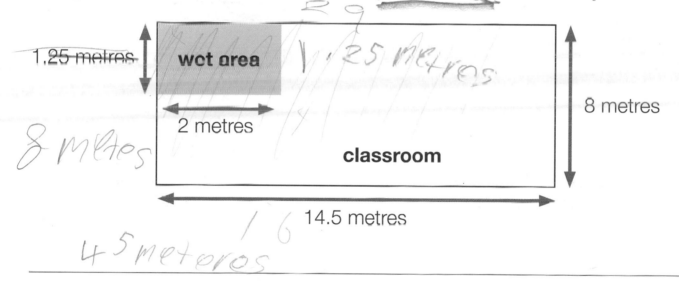

1.25 metres

wct area

1.25 metres

2 metres

8 metres

classroom

14.5 metres

8 metros

45 meteros

_____

_____

2. How much carpet do they need to cover all of the classroom except the wet area?

_____ *113.5* _____

_____

Reading rulers

Read the length of the worms to the nearest millimetre. In each case, the tip of the worm's tail is at the 0cm mark on the ruler.

When measuring these worms it might help to put a piece of paper vertically, in line with the end of the worm and the ruler, to be able to read the measurement more clearly.

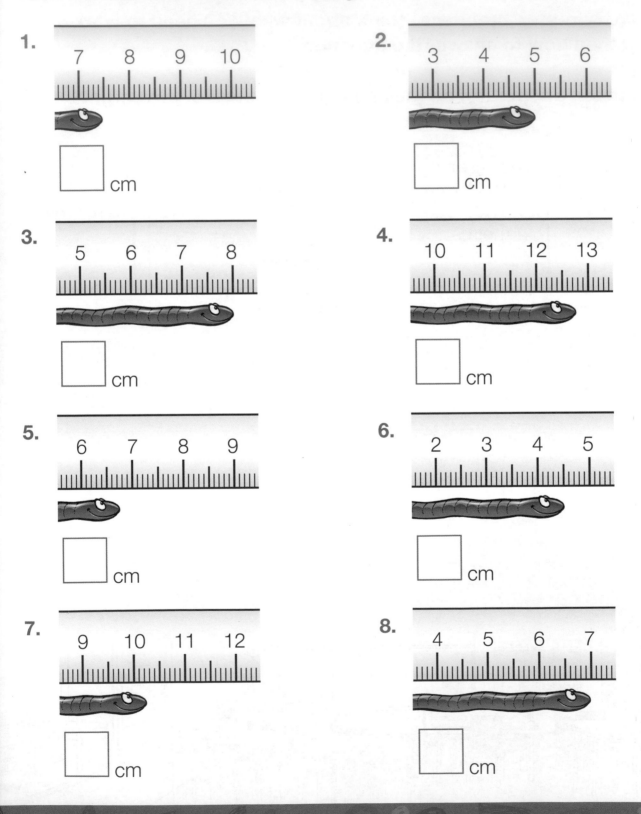

1.
7   8   9   10

☐ cm

2.
3   4   5   6

☐ cm

3.
5   6   7   8

☐ cm

4.
10   11   12   13

☐ cm

5.
6   7   8   9

☐ cm

6.
2   3   4   5

☐ cm

7.
9   10   11   12

☐ cm

8.
4   5   6   7

☐ cm

Ordering and converting mass

When estimating where things go on a number line or scale, first work out the value of each division on the scale. It might then help to estimate where each 100 division would go, before placing the 'in between' amounts.

1. On the number line below, mark your estimate of where the following measurements would go. Write your measurements above the number line.

150g   375g   580g   850g   990g

0kg   1kg

2. Write these masses in kilograms as a decimal.

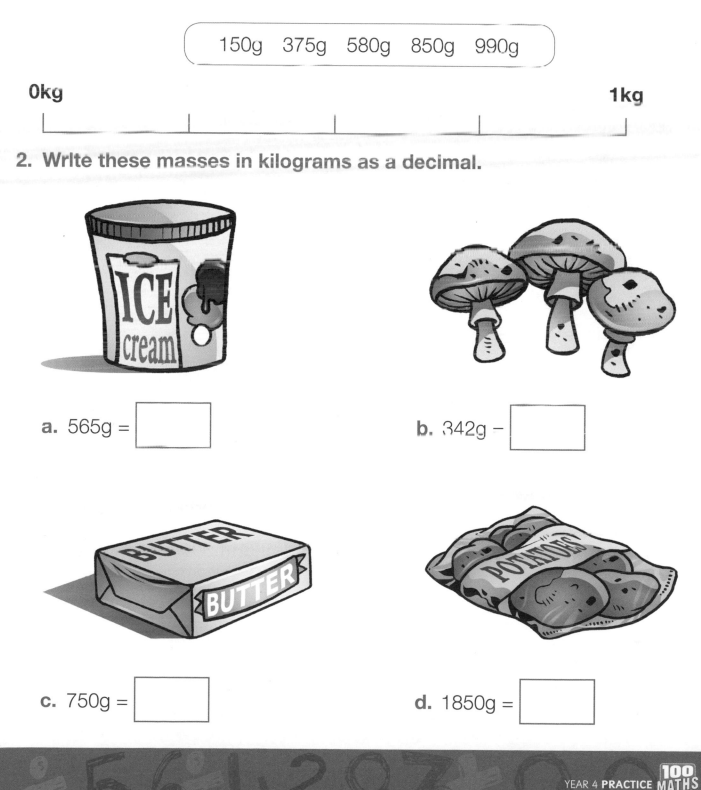

a. 565g = ▢

b. 342g − ▢

c. 750g = ▢

d. 1850g = ▢

Estimating and measuring capacity

1. Ask an adult for permission and some help to find the capacity of some household items.

   Estimate and measure, in millilitres, the capacity of the following items using water and a measuring jug.

   If you don't have an item on the list, cross it out and write in another, similar item.

   Look at your measuring jug and its scale. Use this to help you estimate the capacity of the other containers.

   Remember: 1000ml = 1 litre 500ml = 0.5 litres 250ml = 0.25 litres

Item	Estimate in millilitres	Capacity in millilitres	Capacity in litres
A cup			
A mug			
A small bowl			
A small saucepan			
An empty carton or tin			

2. Now look in your food cupboard or fridge to see if there are any packets or bottles with the capacity written on them.

   Look for a bottle that holds between 100ml and 500ml.

   Write the details below.

   _____

   _____

Analogue and digital times

To tell the time on an analogue clock:

Look at the long hand to count the minutes.

Look at the short hand to find the hour.

Times on a digital clock show the hour and the number of minutes past the hour.
For example, 2:37 is 37 minutes past 2.

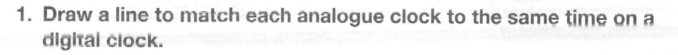

1. **Draw a line to match each analogue clock to the same time on a digital clock.**

12.13

9.08

6.27

5.42

7.36   **3.41**

11.59

6.23

4.24

2.07

Time problems

To find out how many minutes there are in 2 hours 40 minutes, first convert the hours to minutes. Remember, 60 minutes = 1 hour. There are 2 whole hours = 120 minutes. Then add to this number of minutes the 40 minutes you had to start with. 120 minutes + 40 minutes = 160 minutes. So 2 hours 40 minutes = 160 minutes.

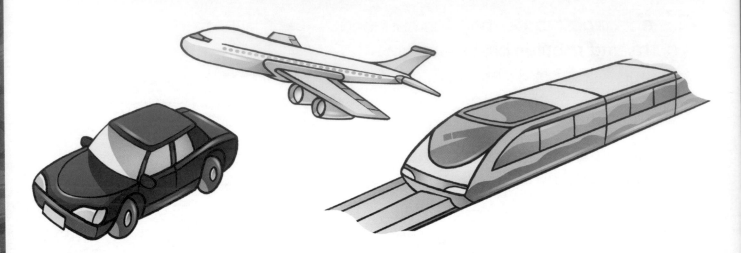

Answer these questions and show how you worked them out.

1. There are 60 seconds in one minute. How many seconds are there in five minutes?

    _____

    _____

2. There are 60 minutes in one hour. How many minutes are there in 3 hours and 50 minutes?

    _____

    _____

3. How many minutes are there in twelve hours and 30 minutes?

    _____

    _____

Magical money problems

The wizard is going to the shop to buy ingredients for his potions. Help him work out the answers to his shopping problems.

Read each problem and decide whether it is an addition, subtraction, multiplication or division problem.

Write a number sentence to match the problem and then work out the answer.

1. One bar of Magic Sludge costs 45p. How many bars could he buy for £3?

   _____

2. The wizard has £25 to spend on a new cauldron. Cauldrons come in three sizes.

   Large £17.50   Medium £14.25   Small £9.75

   How much change would he have if he bought:

   a. the small cauldron? _____

   b. the medium cauldron? _____

   c. the large cauldron? _____

3. The wizard needs the following ingredients:
   Worm Treacle £2.70   4 Droodel Bugs 55p each   3 Gob Rotters 26p each

   a. How much would the ingredients cost altogether? _____

   b. How much change would he have from £6? _____

Measures problems

Read each problem. Decide whether it is an addition, subtraction, multiplication or division problem. Does it require more than one step? Write number sentences for each problem and calculate the answer.

1. Nick is 86cm tall. Paul is 18cm taller.
   How tall is Paul in metres?

_____

_____

_____

2. A rectangle has one side which is 25cm and another side which is 15cm.
   What is its perimeter?

_____

_____

3. A carpenter has a piece of wood that is four metres in length. He cuts off
   90cm of wood. How long is the piece of wood now?

_____

_____

4. Two metres of string is cut into eight equal lengths. How long is each length
   of string?

_____

_____

Perimeter problems

The children at Deepham Primary School have been designing some playground games. Write the answer to each question.

These problems require more than one step to solve them. Write the number sentences needed to solve each step of the problem, then solve it. Make sure you use the same unit of measurement for each part of a problem.

1. Each square on this ladder has sides that are 25cm long. What is the perimeter of the whole ladder?

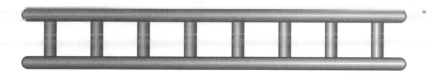

_____

_____

_____

2. The children at school measured the side of a square as 2m 40cm. How many 30cm rulers would be needed to outline the perimeter of the square?

_____

_____

_____

3. One side of this pitch is 10.5m long, while the other is 12.5m long. What is the total distance around the pitch?

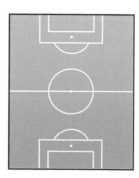

_____

_____

_____

Sorting quadrilaterals

A quadrilateral is any 4-sided shape.

A parallelogram is a quadrilateral with opposite sides that are parallel and equal in length.

A rhombus is a parallelogram with four equal sides and opposite angles that are equal.

A trapezium is a quadrilateral with two parallel sides.

1. Match the shapes to their type.

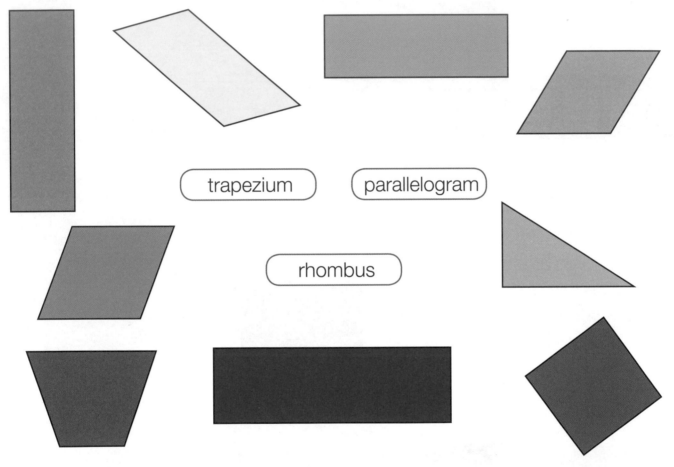

2. Put a tick next to the shapes that fit into more than one type.

3. Explain why some shapes sort into two types.

_____

_____

Classifying quadrilaterals

Read again the definitions of different types of quadrilateral on page 104. Remember that any 4-sided shape is a quadrilateral.

A square is the only regular quadrilateral because it is the only one whose sides and angles are all the same size.

A shape is symmetrical if you can fold it in half exactly and both sides are the same.

1. **Draw four 4-sided shapes on the isometric paper below.**

2. **Number each shape, then fill out the table to classify each of your shapes.**

Number of shape	Regular or irregular?	How many lines of symmetry?	How many right angles?	Name of shape
1				
2				
3				
4				

Sorting triangles

There are different types of triangle:

- Right-angled triangle – a 3-sided shape with one right angle.
- Isosceles triangle – a 3-sided shape with 2 equal-length sides and 2 equal angles.
- Equilateral triangle – a 3-sided shape with all sides and angles equal.
- Scalene triangle – a 3-sided shape with no sides or angles equal.

1. **Sort the triangles into the correct section of the Carroll diagram by writing the letter in the correct box.**

	Right-angled triangle	Not a right-angled triangle
Isosceles triangle		
Not an isosceles triangle		

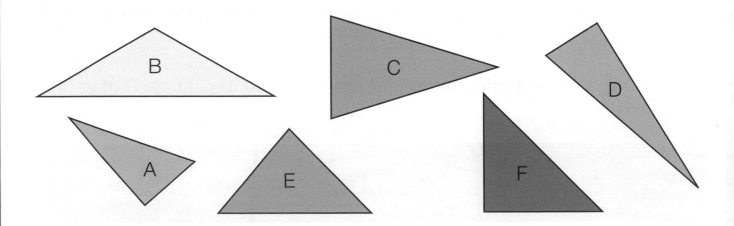

2. **Complete these sentences.**

   a. A scalene triangle does not _____

   b. An equilateral triangle _____

Classifying triangles

Remember that a triangle is any 3-sided shape. There are different types of triangles: right-angled, equilateral, isosceles and scalene.

An equilateral triangle is the only regular triangle because it is the only one whose sides and angles are all the same size.

A triangle is symmetrical if you can fold it in half exactly and both sides are the same.

1. Draw four different types of triangle on the isometric paper below.

2. Number each triangle, then fill out the table to classify each of your shapes.

Number of triangle	Regular or irregular?	How many lines of symmetry?	How many right angles?	Name of shape
1				
2				
3				
4				

Angles in shapes

Regular shapes have all sides of equal length and all angles of equal size. Irregular shapes have sides that are not equal in length and angles that are not equal in size.

Angles and sides equal = **regular**.

Angles and sides not equal = **irregular**.

1. **Using tracing paper and a ruler, compare the sides and angles of each shape and write the correct label.**

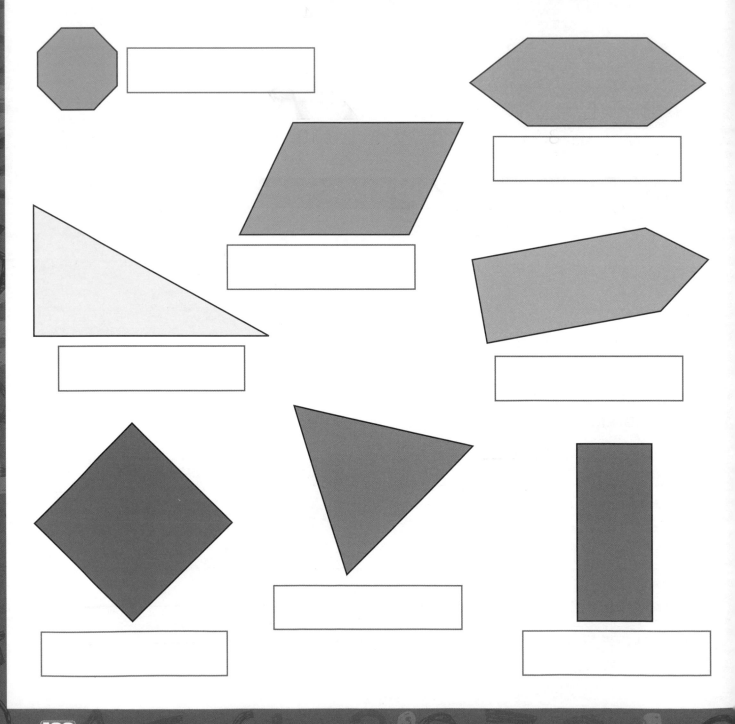

Sorting shapes

You can use a mirror to find the lines of symmetry in a shape. A shape is symmetrical if you can fold it in half exactly and both sides are the same.

1. Look at each shape and complete the table.

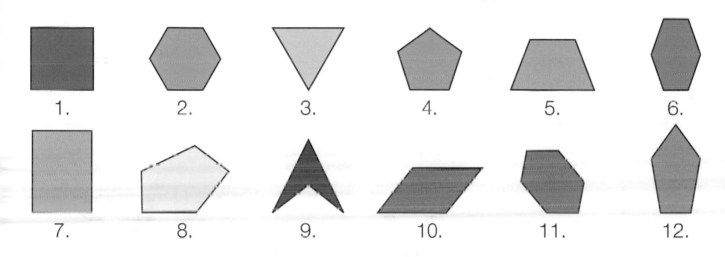

Shape	Regular or irregular shape?	Name of shape	Number of lines of symmetry
1			
2			
3			
4			
5			
6			
7			
8			
9			
10			
11			
12			

Shape sifting

Remember: regular shapes, or polygons, have all sides and angles equal. If a shape has two or more lines of symmetry, you must be able to find two different ways to fold it in half exactly.

1. Tick the polygons that are irregular.

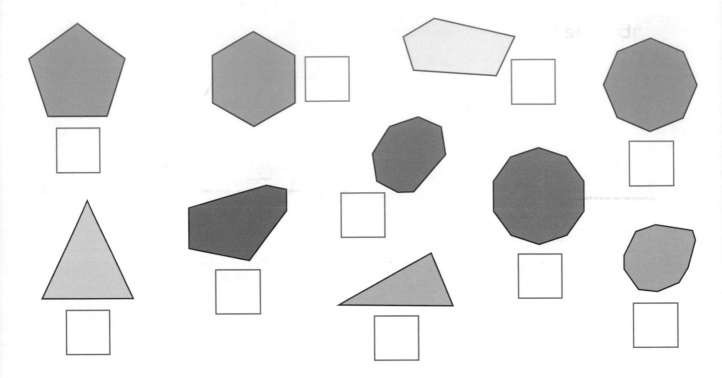

2. Tick the shapes that have two lines of symmetry.

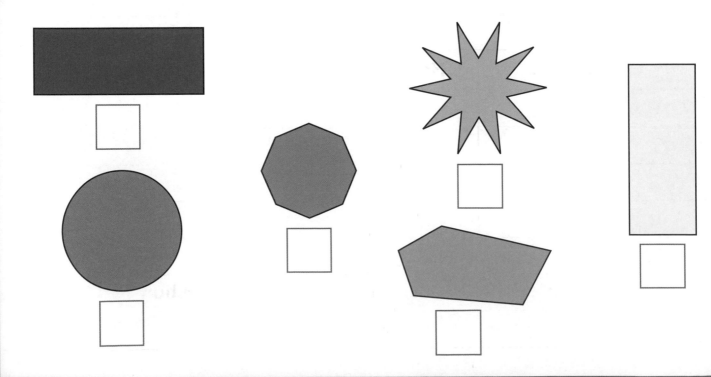

Order and compare angles

Look at these angles.

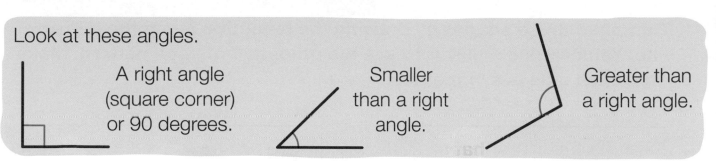

A right angle
(square corner)
or 90 degrees.

Smaller
than a right
angle.

Greater than
a right angle.

1. **Number the boxes 1 to 8 in order, starting with the smallest angle.**

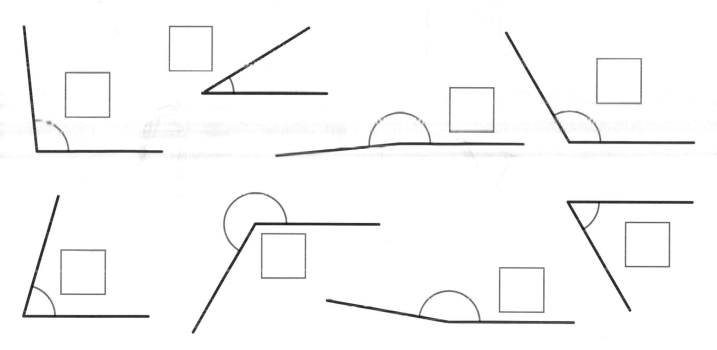

2. **Draw an angle to match the description in each box below.**

A right angle	Half a right angle	Half of 360 degrees

3. **How would these fit into your ordered angles in question 1?**

_____

Mirror, mirror

1. Complete these shapes by drawing the reflection along the mirror line. You can use a mirror to see the other half of each pattern. Make sure each side is symmetrical.

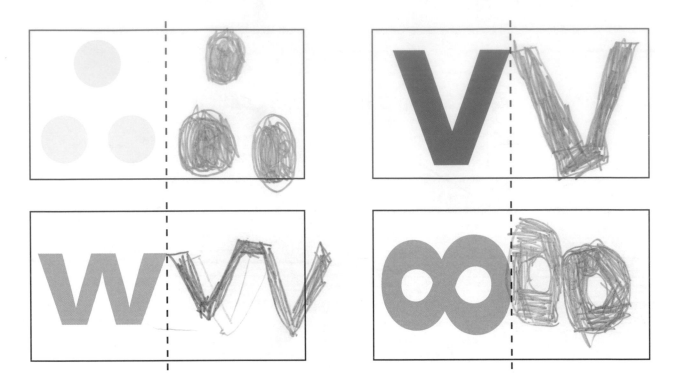

2. Draw the other half of each of these sea creatures. Each half should match exactly.

Drawing mirror images

1. Draw the mirror image for each of these.

    Use a mirror and stand it vertically on the line of symmetry to see the mirror image. It will help if you count how many squares from the symmetry line your shape needs to be.

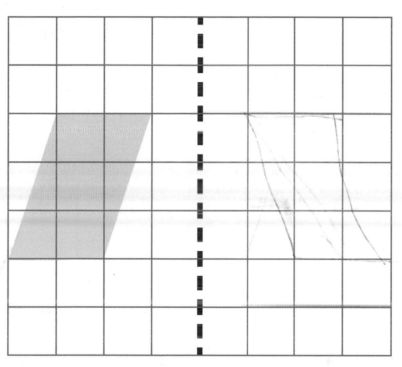

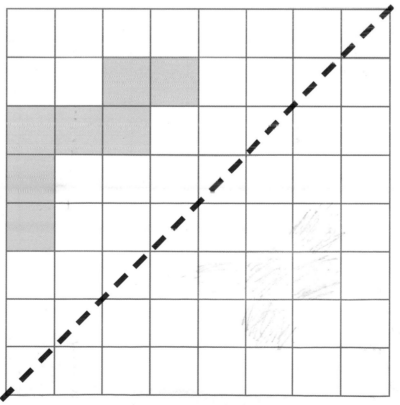

Mystery picture coordinates

To plot a coordinate, such as (5,8), start with the 5: read along the bottom axis until you get to 5. Then read up the left axis until you get to 8. Put a cross where the lines meet. This is the point (5,8).

Remember, first go across, then go up.

1. **Draw a picture by plotting the coordinates and joining each point to the next with a straight line.**

    (1,0); (3,2); (3,5); (3,8); (5,10); (7,8); (7,5); (7,2); (9,0); (7,0); (7,1); (6,1); (6,0); (4,0); (4,1); (3,1); (3,0); join the last point to the first.

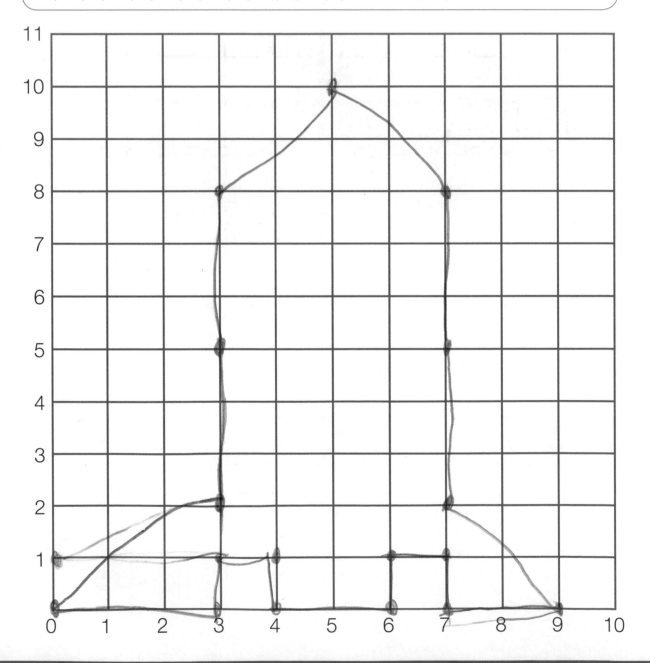

Mystery picture coordinates

Remember, when writing pairs of coordinates, the first number is read along the bottom axis, and the second number is read along the left axis.

1. **Design your own picture. Write down the coordinates for it, so that someone else could draw the picture from your instructions. Each point on your picture will need a new pair of coordinates.**

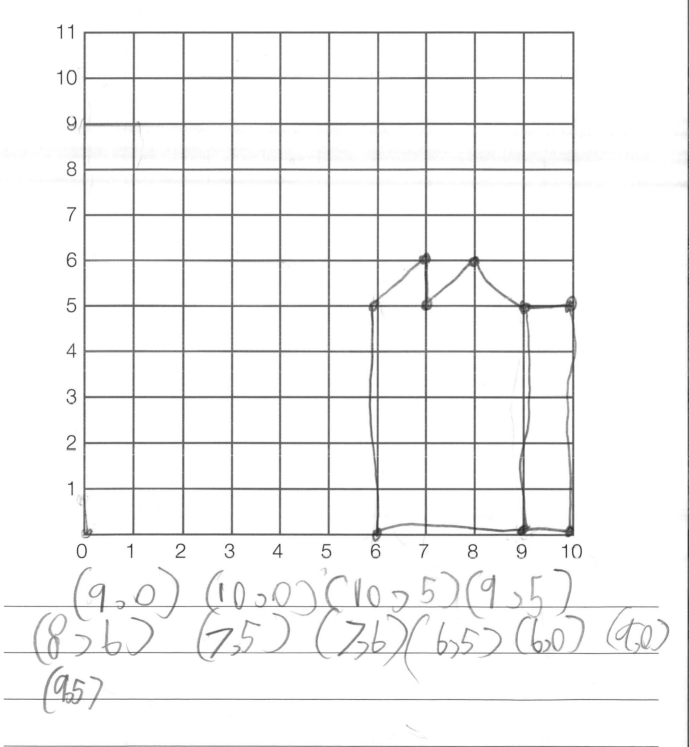

$(9,0)$ $(10,0)$ $(10,5)$ $(9,5)$
$(8,6)$ $(7,5)$ $(7,6)(6,5)$ $(6,0)$ $(9,0)$
$(9,5)$

Plotting shapes

1. **Plot the 4-sided shapes given by these coordinates. Mark each pair of coordinates with a small cross, then join up each one using a ruler. Use a different colour to plot each shape.**

   (x,y)

   Shape A: (4,1); (5,3); (8,3); (8,1), join the last point to the first.

   Shape B: (10,5); (11,5); (12,3); (10,3), join the last point to the first.

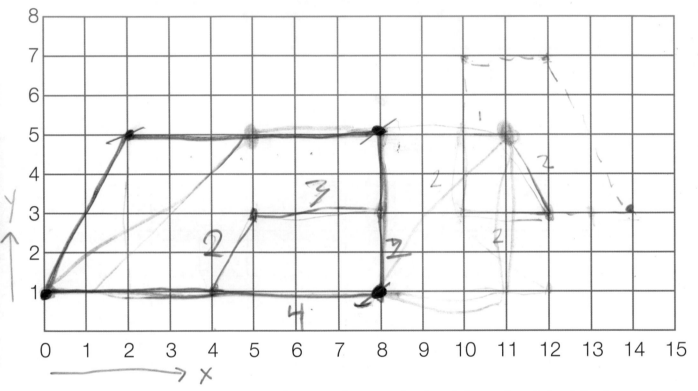

2. **The shapes above are going to have their sides doubled in length.**

   a. Plot the new shapes on the grid. Use a different colour for each shape.

   b. Write the coordinates for each shape.

(10,3) (10,7) (12,7) (14,3)

(8,1) (2,5) (8,9) (0,17)

Shapes and coordinates

Read the clue to each shape carefully. Draw the shapes on the grid.
Think about how big each shape needs to be, before you draw it.
After drawing each shape, work out the coordinates for each corner.
Remember to write the coordinates like this: (*x*-axis, *y*-axis).

1. I am a square with sides of length 4cm.

_____

2. I am a rectangle with a perimeter of 20cm.

_____

3. I am a rectangle with an area of 15cm².

_____

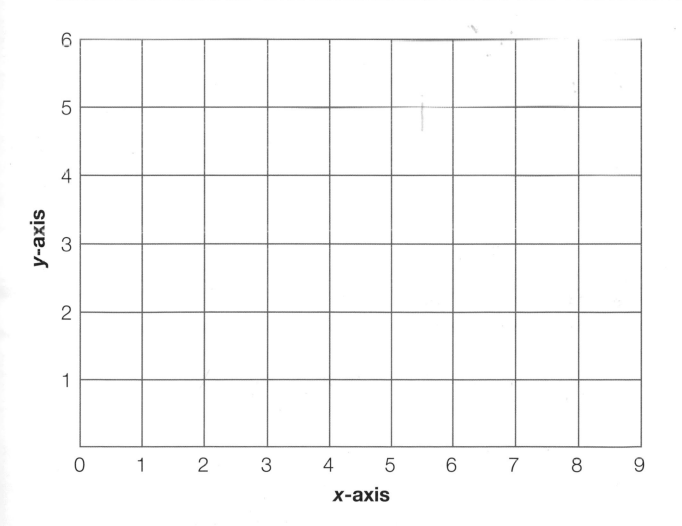

Directions

When giving directions, use these words: north, south, east and west. On a grid, remember to count the number of squares moved each time.

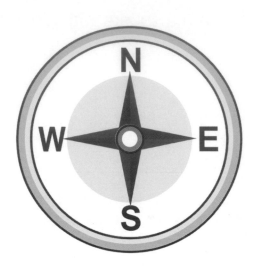

Look at the above grid. What directions do you need to give:

1. for the blackbird to catch the fly?

_____

2. for the duck to eat the dragonfly?

_____

3. for the ladybird to land at the top of the most easterly bulrush?

_____

4. for the blackbird to eat the earwig, the dragonfly, the ladybird and the fly?

_____

_____

Describe translations

A translation is when you move an object in any direction, without flipping or rotating it. When you move an object, describe its movement using these words: left or right, up or down.

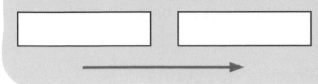

The rectangle has moved to the right.

Describe the movement of each of these shapes.

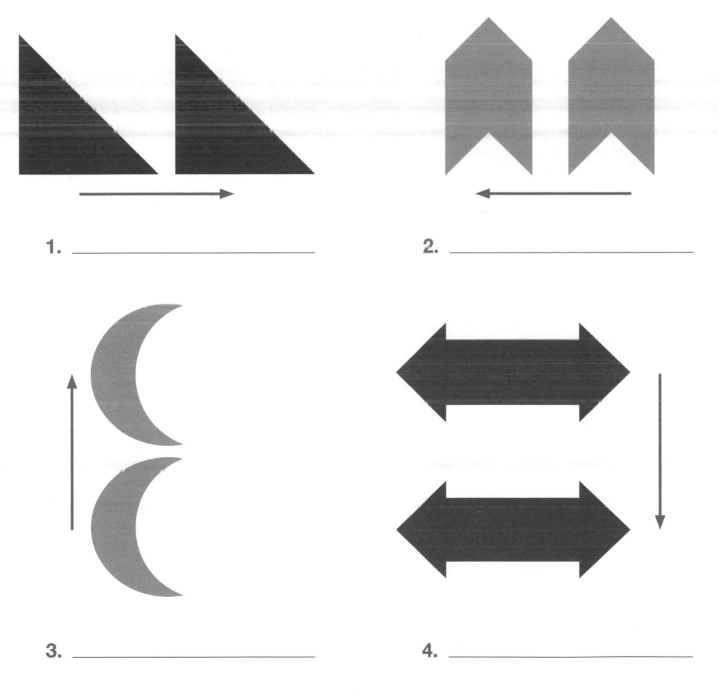

1. _____

2. _____

3. _____

4. _____

Favourite days bar chart

To understand a bar chart, look at the scale and decide what each rectangle, or part rectangle, represents.

Look at the labels for each axis and the heading of the graph. All this information will help you to answer questions about the bar chart.

Look at this bar chart and answer the following questions.

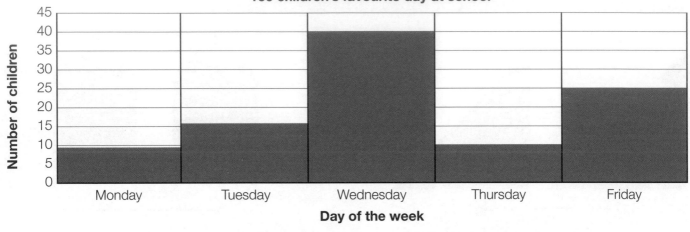

1. How many children took part in the survey? _____

2. What was the favourite day of the week? _____

3. Which day of the week did ten children vote for? _____

4. What is the difference between the number of votes for Thursday and the number of votes for Wednesday?

   _____

5. Why do you think Wednesday could be a popular day of the week?

   _____

6. If 16 children voted Tuesday as their favourite day of the week, how many children voted Monday as their favourite day?

   _____

Drawing a bar chart

The table below shows how many people came to the Lunch Counter restaurant during one week.

Mon	Tues	Wed	Thurs	Fri	Sat	Sun
60	55	15	80	25	90	45

1. Draw a bar chart to show this information. Look at the scale on the bar chart and decide how to represent the information. Write what you think would be the best title for this bar chart.

Title: _____

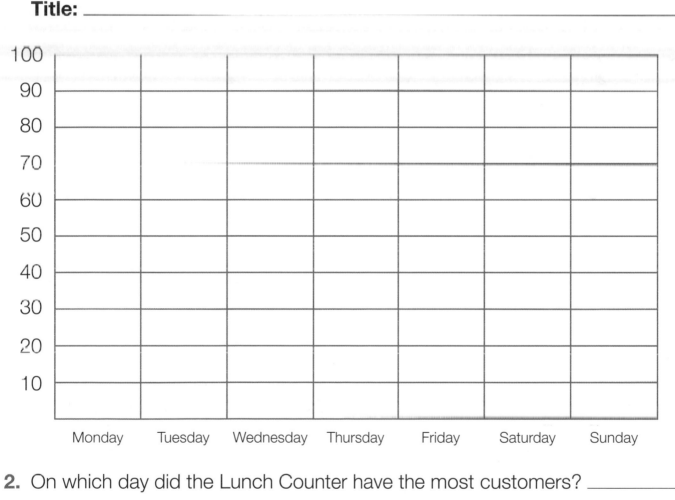

2. On which day did the Lunch Counter have the most customers? _____

3. Which was the least busy day? _____

4. Which two days had a total of 145 customers? _____

5. How many customers were there over the weekend? _____

Interpret information in a time graph

Time graphs show changes in something over a period of time. Look at the scale on the graph to see how much each division is worth.

This time graph shows a baby's weight over 6 months. You could work out the increase each month first to make it easier to answer the questions.

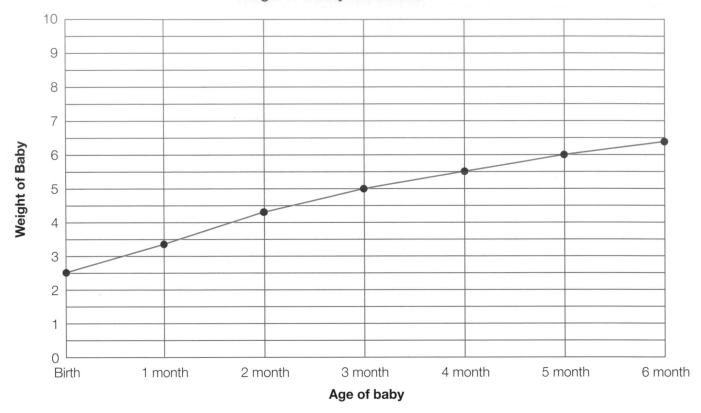

Weight of a Baby 0–6 months.

1. What is the baby's weight at 2 months? _____

2. What was the increase in weight between birth and 3 months? _____

3. Which month showed the greatest increase in weight? _____

4. Which month showed the smallest increase in weight? _____

5. What was the baby's total weight gain during the 6 months? _____

6. The baby does not gain the same amount of weight each month.

   Give a possible explanation for this. _____

Drawing a time graph

To plot the information from this table on a time graph, first find the week at the bottom of your graph and run your finger up the line until it meets the line for the correct number of centimetres. Draw a small cross where the lines meet. You can later join all the crosses to make your line graph.

1. Use the data in the table to create a time graph. Choose the best scale for your graph.

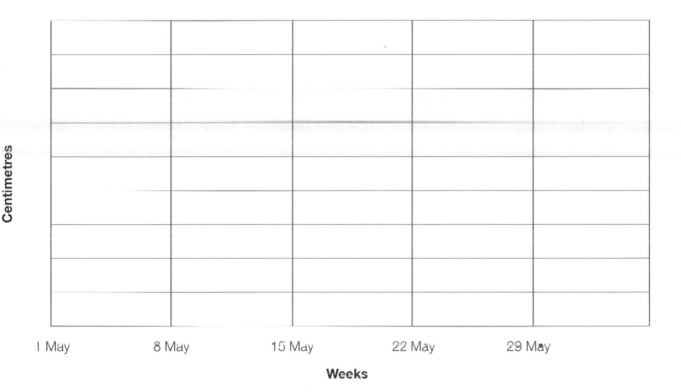

Weeks

Sweet Pea growth during May

Week beginning	1 May	8 May	15 May	22 May	29 May
Height in cm	6	15	22	32	41

2. Which week showed the greatest growth? _____

3. Which week showed the least growth? _____

4. What was the total growth during May? _____

Workout pictograms

This pictogram shows the number of hours of exercise 100 children took in one week.

1. Fill in the '4 hours or more' row. Remember that all the rows must add up to 100 in total.

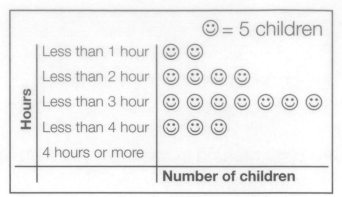

Hours	☺ = 5 children						
Less than 1 hour	☺	☺					
Less than 2 hour	☺	☺	☺	☺			
Less than 3 hour	☺	☺	☺	☺	☺	☺	☺
Less than 4 hour	☺	☺	☺				
4 hours or more							

Number of children

2. Now, using the data in the pictogram, complete the blank pictogram below to represent the same data using the scale ☺ = 10 children. Remember that you may have to use half a ☺ to represent 5 children.

Tip: Make a note of the total number of children for each section. This information will help when completing the first pictogram, and can be used to help you create the second pictogram.

☺= 10 children

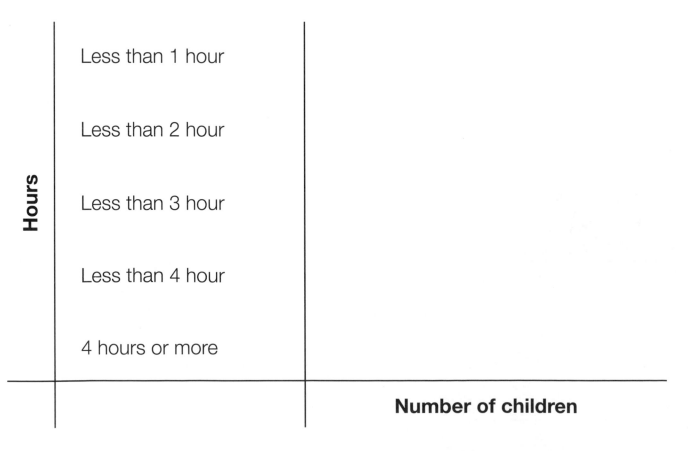

Hours	
Less than 1 hour	
Less than 2 hour	
Less than 3 hour	
Less than 4 hour	
4 hours or more	

Number of children

Presenting data

Tip: Remember, when reading tally charts, ⅢⅡ = 5.

Tony made a tally chart to show the wildlife he spotted in the woods near his house in one day.

Animal	Number
Pigeon	ⅢⅡ ⅢⅡ ⅢⅡ ⅢⅡ ⅢⅡ ⅢⅡ ⅢⅡ |||
Fox	ⅢⅡ	
Rabbit	ⅢⅡ ⅢⅡ ⅢⅡ ⅢⅡ ||
Badger	|||
Deer	ⅢⅡ

1. Decide how you could present this information, in a block graph, a bar chart or a pictogram. Draw your graph in the space below.
   First work out the totals for each of the animals. This will help you to decide on a scale for your graph.
   Remember to label each axis and give your graph a title.

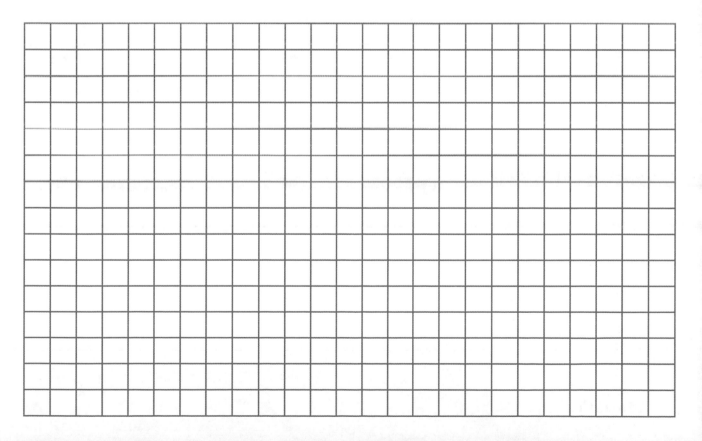

Progress chart

Making progress? Tick (✔) the flower boxes as you complete each section of the book.

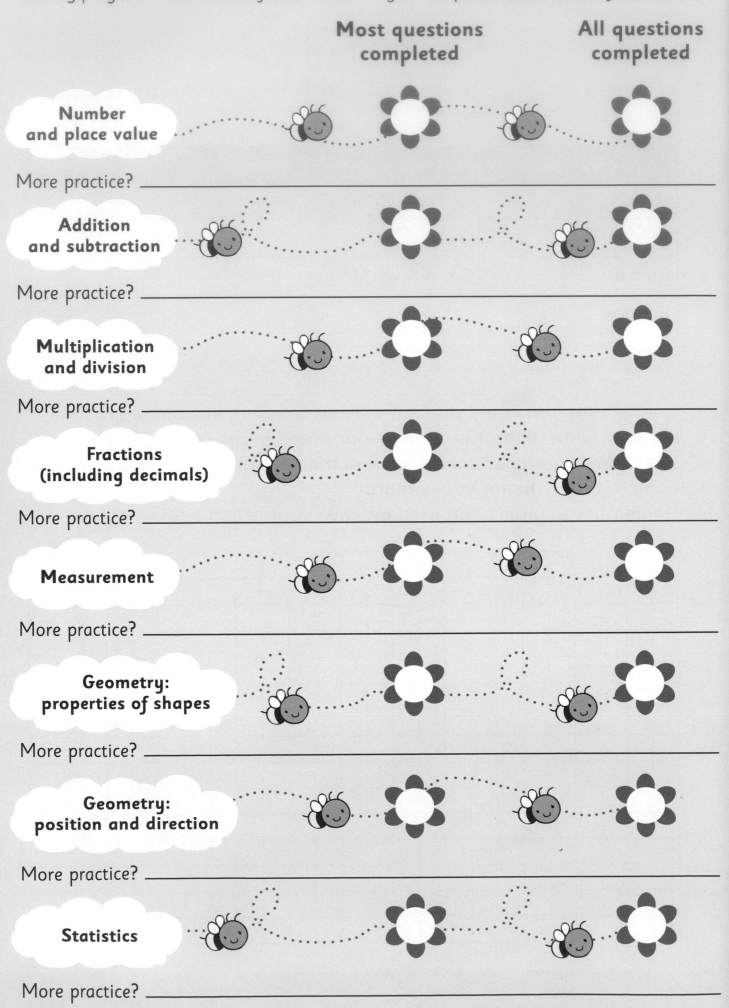

Most questions completed

All questions completed

Number and place value

More practice? _____

Addition and subtraction

More practice? _____

Multiplication and division

More practice? _____

Fractions (including decimals)

More practice? _____

Measurement

More practice? _____

Geometry: properties of shapes

More practice? _____

Geometry: position and direction

More practice? _____

Statistics

More practice? _____

Index